THE OLD
FARMER'S
ALMANAC

VEGETABLE
GARDENER'S
HANDBOOK

The Old Farmer's Almanac Books
PUBLISHER: Sherin Pierce
EDITOR: Janice Stillman
CREATIVE DIRECTOR: Colleen Quinnell
MANAGING EDITOR: Jack Burnett
EDITORIAL STAFF: Tim Goodwin, Sarah Perreault, Heidi Stonehill

V.P., NEW MEDIA AND PRODUCTION: Paul Belliveau
PRODUCTION DIRECTOR: David Ziarnowski
PRODUCTION MANAGER: Brian Johnson
SENIOR PRODUCTION ARTISTS: Jennifer Freeman, Rachel Kipka
SENIOR AD PRODUCTION COORDINATOR: Janet Selle

SENIOR DIGITAL EDITOR: Catherine Boeckmann
DIGITAL EDITOR: Christopher Burnett
SENIOR WEB DESIGNER: Amy O'Brien
DIGITAL MARKETING SPECIALISTS: Jessica Garcia, Holly Sanderson
E-MAIL MARKETING SPECIALIST: Eric Bailey
E-COMMERCE MARKETING DIRECTOR: Alan Henning
PROGRAMMING: Reinvented, Inc.

CONTRIBUTORS: Brian Bell, Margaret Boyles, Brook Elliott, GrowVeg.com, Doreen G. Howard, Mare-Anne Jarvela, Robert Kaldenbach, Martie Majoros, Georgia Orcutt, Melissa Pace, Susan Peery, Robin Sweetser, Gayla Trail, Cynthia Van Hazinga, Jon Vara

COVER AND TITLE PAGE PHOTO CREDITS: See individual vegetable chapters.
BACK COVER PHOTOS, CLOCKWISE FROM TOP LEFT: Prostock-studio/Shutterstock; AlexRaths/Getty Images; cjp/Getty Images; fotokostic/Getty Images; firina/Getty Images; Nobilior/Getty Images

For additional information about this and other publications from The Old Farmer's Almanac, visit ALMANAC.COM or call 1-800-ALMANAC.

Distributed in the book trade by HarperCollins in the United States and by Firefly Books Ltd. in Canada.

Yankee Publishing Inc., P.O. Box 520, 1121 Main Street, Dublin, New Hampshire 03444

Thank you for buying this book! Thanks, too, to everyone who had a hand in it, including Morgan Hillman, printers, distributors, and sales people.

ISBN: 978-1-57198-845-4
Sixth Edition

Printed in China by C. J. Printing Media Co.

THE OLD
FARMER'S
ALMANAC

VEGETABLE
GARDENER'S
HANDBOOK

CONTENTS

PART 1

CONTENTS
PART 2

VEGETABLES

GROWING CONCERNS

GROUND RULES

GETTING STARTED

LIFE BEGINS THE DAY YOU START A GARDEN.
—Chinese proverb

Whether you're starting a new garden or extending an existing one, give careful consideration to where you site it.

CHOOSE A SUNNY SPOT
Most vegetables need at least 6 hours of sunlight per day, although some crops, such as broccoli, lettuce, spinach, and other greens, will grow well in spaces with more shade. In general, the more sunlight vegetables receive, the greater the harvest and the better the taste.

BE IN THE CLEAR
Avoid planting crops near large trees. These will not only cast shade but also compete with your vegetables for nutrients and water. Also, soil near walls and fences and under overhanging trees tends to be too dry for good plant growth; an open area is best.

KNOW YOUR WATER WAYS AND MEANS
Have water readily available. Hand watering, with a hose or watering can, is likely to be necessary during dry weather. (Sprinklers are fun but waste a lot of water.)

If you think that water will be an ongoing challenge, consider installing a soaker or drip hose. Soaker hoses and drip irrigation use a fraction of the water used by a sprinkler and deliver the water where it is needed. Keeping foliage dry has the added benefit of reducing disease problems.

ENCOURAGE AIR TRAVEL
Good airflow will encourage sturdy growth in your plants and help to keep diseases at bay. It also makes the garden less hospitable to insect pests such as whiteflies, which prefer a stagnant, humid environment.

BE WARY OF THE WINDS OF CHANGE
Solid walls or fences may provide shelter, but they can also cause the wind to form destructive turbulence on the leeward side, so do not plant too close to them. Hedges and open or woven fences are more effective, as they filter wind rather than deflect it. Shelter from winds is helpful for most crops, especially peppers, eggplant, peas, beans, and any climbing vegetables.

AVOID A SPACE RACE
The size of your garden really depends on the space available in an area that gets 6 to 8 hours of sunlight. Consider the amount of space that you have and which vegetables you want to grow. Some vegetables require more space to grow than others. For example, corn needs a lot of space and can overshadow smaller vegetables.

Plants set too close together compete for sunlight, water, and nutrition and fail to mature. Not enough space? Grow vegetables in containers. Remember: It's better to be proud of a small garden than to be frustrated with a big one!

WARM TO BEING FROST-FREE

Cold air is heavier than warm air, so it settles in low points in the garden and near structures such as walls and fences. Avoid planting in these potential frost pockets; doing so can delay the time when you can start to sow seeds, as well as lead to damage in young growth.

The last frost in spring and first frost in fall will also affect your success: If the season is not long enough, your plants may not reach maturity. Our U.S. and Canadian Frosts and Growing Seasons tables can help you to determine the growing season in your area. For the first and last frost dates in selected areas, turn to pages 12–13; for dates specific to your own city or town, visit Almanac.com/frostdates.

U.S. FROSTS AND GROWING SEASONS

Dates given are normal averages for a light freeze; local weather and topography may cause considerable variations. The possibility of frost occurring after the spring dates and before the fall dates is 30 percent. The classification of freeze temperatures is usually based on their effect on plants. **Light freeze:** 29° to 32°F—tender plants killed. **Moderate freeze:** 25° to 28°F—widely destructive to most plants. **Severe freeze:** 24°F and colder—heavy damage to most plants.

–dates courtesy of National Centers for Environmental Information

STATE	CITY	GROWING SEASON (DAYS)	LAST SPRING FROST	FIRST FALL FROST	STATE	CITY	GROWING SEASON (DAYS)	LAST SPRING FROST	FIRST FALL FROST
AK	Juneau	171	Apr. 26	Oct. 15	NC	Fayetteville	212	Apr. 5	Nov. 4
AL	Mobile	269	Mar. 3	Nov. 28	ND	Bismarck	126	May 19	Sept. 23
AR	Pine Bluff	230	Mar. 22	Nov. 8	NE	Omaha	174	Apr. 23	Oct. 15
AZ	Phoenix	354*	Jan. 9	Dec. 30	NE	North Platte	131	May 16	Sept. 25
AZ	Tucson	309*	Feb. 2	Dec. 9	NH	Concord	136	May 15	Sept. 29
CA	Eureka	268	Mar. 4	Nov. 28	NJ	Newark	211	Apr. 6	Nov. 4
CA	Sacramento	281*	Feb. 17	Nov. 26	NM	Carlsbad	223	Mar. 27	Nov. 6
CO	Denver	154	May 4	Oct. 6	NM	Los Alamos	149	May 9	Oct. 6
CO	Grand Junction	159	May 3	Oct. 10	NV	Las Vegas	292*	Feb. 11	Dec. 1
CT	Hartford	165	Apr. 27	Oct. 10	NY	Albany	159	May 2	Oct. 9
DE	Wilmington	199	Apr. 13	Oct. 30	NY	Syracuse	158	May 5	Oct. 11
FL	Orlando	337*	Jan. 30	Jan. 3**	OH	Akron	174	Apr. 30	Oct. 22
FL	Tallahassee	238	Mar. 19	Nov. 13	OH	Cincinnati	179	Apr. 23	Oct. 20
GA	Athens	217	Mar. 31	Nov. 4	OK	Lawton	206	Apr. 7	Oct. 31
GA	Savannah	253	Mar. 12	Nov. 21	OK	Tulsa	207	Apr. 5	Oct. 30
IA	Atlantic	142	May 6	Sept. 26	OR	Pendleton	155	Apr. 30	Oct. 3
IA	Cedar Rapids	155	May 4	Oct. 7	OR	Portland	260	Mar. 6	Nov. 22
ID	Boise	166	Apr. 30	Oct. 14	PA	Franklin	160	May 9	Oct. 17
IL	Chicago	193	Apr. 17	Oct. 28	PA	Williamsport	167	May 1	Oct. 16
IL	Springfield	177	Apr. 20	Oct. 15	RI	Kingston	148	May 8	Oct. 4
IN	Indianapolis	172	Apr. 26	Oct. 16	SC	Charleston	305*	Feb. 17	Dec. 20
IN	South Bend	159	May 7	Oct. 14	SC	Columbia	235	Mar. 21	Nov. 12
KS	Topeka	182	Apr. 19	Oct. 19	SD	Rapid City	144	May 9	Oct. 1
KY	Lexington	185	Apr. 20	Oct. 23	TN	Memphis	229	Mar. 24	Nov. 9
LA	Monroe	238	Mar. 14	Nov. 8	TN	Nashville	206	Apr. 6	Oct. 30
LA	New Orleans	311*	Feb. 8	Dec. 17	TX	Amarillo	184	Apr. 20	Oct. 22
MA	Boston	208	Apr. 8	Nov. 3	TX	Denton	235	Mar. 21	Nov. 12
MA	Worcester	167	Apr. 29	Oct. 14	TX	San Antonio	267	Mar. 2	Nov. 25
MD	Baltimore	192	Apr. 16	Oct. 26	UT	Cedar City	119	May 31	Sept. 28
ME	Portland	160	May 1	Oct. 9	UT	Spanish Fork	162	May 2	Oct. 12
MI	Lansing	151	May 7	Oct. 6	VA	Norfolk	239	Mar. 23	Nov. 18
MI	Marquette	152	May 15	Oct. 15	VA	Richmond	204	Apr. 9	Oct. 31
MN	Duluth	129	May 19	Sept. 26	VT	Burlington	158	May 3	Oct. 9
MN	Willmar	149	May 4	Oct. 1	WA	Seattle	246	Mar. 12	Nov. 14
MO	Jefferson City	193	Apr. 14	Oct. 25	WA	Spokane	158	May 1	Oct. 7
MS	Columbia	243	Mar. 13	Nov. 12	WI	Green Bay	148	May 7	Oct. 3
MS	Tupelo	218	Mar. 30	Nov. 4	WI	Sparta	133	May 15	Sept. 26
MT	Fort Peck	135	May 13	Sept. 26	WV	Parkersburg	186	Apr. 20	Oct. 24
MT	Helena	132	May 15	Sept. 25	WY	Casper	105	June 1	Sept. 15

*In leap years, add 1 day   **In following year

CANADIAN FROSTS AND GROWING SEASONS

Dates given are normal averages for a light freeze; local weather and topography may cause considerable variations. The possibility of frost occurring after the spring dates and before the fall dates is 33 percent. The classification of freeze temperatures is usually based on their effect on plants. **Light freeze:** –2° to 0°C (29° to 32°F)—tender plants killed. **Moderate freeze:** –4° to –2°C (25° to 28°F)—widely destructive to most plants. **Severe freeze:** –4°C (24°F and colder)—heavy damage to most plants.

–dates courtesy of Environment Canada

PROV.	CITY	GROWING SEASON (DAYS)	LAST SPRING FROST	FIRST FALL FROST	PROV.	CITY	GROWING SEASON (DAYS)	LAST SPRING FROST	FIRST FALL FROST
AB	Athabasca	103	May 28	Sept. 9	NT	Fort Simpson	81	May 31	Aug. 21
AB	Calgary	99	May 29	Sept. 6	NT	Norman Wells	91	May 29	Aug. 29
AB	Edmonton	123	May 15	Sept. 16	NT	Yellowknife	102	May 31	Sept. 11
AB	Grande Prairie	106	May 22	Sept. 6	ON	Barrie	147	May 12	Oct. 7
AB	Lethbridge	113	May 22	Sept. 13	ON	Brantford	151	May 5	Oct. 4
AB	Medicine Hat	118	May 18	Sept. 14	ON	Hamilton	160	May 3	Oct. 11
AB	Peace River	96	May 28	Sept. 2	ON	Kapuskasing	75	June 18	Sept. 2
AB	Red Deer	108	May 24	Sept. 10	ON	Kingston	161	Apr. 28	Oct. 7
BC	Abbotsford	168	Apr. 30	Oct. 16	ON	London	142	May 13	Oct. 3
BC	Castlegar	141	May 8	Sept. 27	ON	Ottawa	135	May 13	Sept. 26
BC	Chilliwack	191	Apr. 19	Oct. 28	ON	Owen Sound	147	May 14	Oct. 9
BC	Coombs	139	May 13	Sept. 30	ON	Peterborough	137	May 12	Sept. 27
BC	Dawson Creek	76	June 8	Aug. 24	ON	Sudbury	124	May 21	Sept. 23
BC	Kamloops	152	May 3	Oct. 3	ON	Timmins	86	June 13	Sept. 8
BC	Kelowna	150	May 8	Oct. 6	ON	Toronto	161	May 4	Oct. 13
BC	Nanaimo	163	May 4	Oct. 15	ON	Wawa	97	June 6	Sept. 12
BC	Prince George	120	May 20	Sept. 18	ON	Windsor	172	Apr. 28	Oct. 18
BC	Prince Rupert	145	May 14	Oct. 7	PE	Alberton	122	May 31	Oct. 1
BC	Vancouver	180	Apr. 21	Oct. 19	PE	Charlottetown	142	May 22	Oct. 12
BC	Victoria	208	Apr. 14	Nov. 9	PE	Summerside	154	May 13	Oct. 15
MB	Brandon	92	June 6	Sept. 7	QC	Baie-Comeau	103	June 2	Sept. 14
MB	Lynn Lake	87	June 10	Sept. 6	QC	La Tuque	101	June 5	Sept. 15
MB	The Pas	106	May 31	Sept. 15	QC	Magog	129	May 19	Sept. 26
MB	Thompson	58	June 18	Aug. 16	QC	Montréal	152	May 6	Oct. 6
MB	Winnipeg	116	May 21	Sept. 15	QC	Québec	129	May 17	Sept. 24
NB	Bathurst	101	June 4	Sept. 14	QC	Rimouski	140	May 18	Oct. 6
NB	Fredericton	125	May 22	Sept. 25	QC	Roberval	117	May 25	Sept. 20
NB	Miramichi	115	May 27	Sept. 20	QC	Thetford Mines	128	May 20	Sept. 26
NB	Moncton	103	June 3	Sept. 15	QC	Trois-Rivières	128	May 19	Sept. 25
NB	Saint John	165	Apr. 30	Oct. 13	SK	Moose Jaw	110	May 24	Sept. 12
NL	Corner Brook	129	May 27	Oct. 4	SK	North Battleford	108	May 26	Sept. 12
NL	Gander	120	June 7	Oct. 6	SK	Prince Albert	88	June 7	Sept. 4
NL	Grand Falls	105	June 8	Sept. 22	SK	Regina	91	June 1	Sept. 1
NL	St. John's	124	June 6	Oct. 9	SK	Saskatoon	126	May 15	Sept. 19
NS	Halifax	164	May 8	Oct. 20	SK	Weyburn	107	May 26	Sept. 11
NS	Kentville	122	May 26	Sept. 26	SK	Yorkton	106	May 26	Sept. 10
NS	Sydney	135	May 27	Oct. 10	YT	Dawson	62	June 9	Aug. 11
NS	Truro	103	June 7	Sept. 19	YT	Watson Lake	83	June 6	Aug. 29
NS	Yarmouth	162	May 4	Oct. 14	YT	Whitehorse	72	June 12	Aug. 24

TOOLS FOR IMPLEMENTING SUCCESS

MAN IS A TOOL-USING ANIMAL. WITHOUT TOOLS, HE IS NOTHING, WITH TOOLS HE IS ALL.
—Thomas Carlyle, Scottish social commentator (1795–1881)

Some tools, implements, and equipment are essential to gardening successfully. Here are the basics:

A **garden fork** is used for turning over soil and compost, digging root crops, and dividing perennials.

Garden scissors are used for deadheading flowers, cutting herbs and flowers, and pruning delicate plants.

Gloves can help to prevent blisters and cuts—and keep your hands clean.

A **hand cultivator** scratches the soil. It is useful for removing small weeds and roughing up the soil, both in the garden and in a container.

A **hand pruner** removes small branches from perennials, shrubs, and trees. Choose a bypass pruner with smooth operating blades and a comfortable grip.

A **hoe** is used to remove shallow-rooted weeds. It is also used to create furrows for planting seed and to break up clumps of soil. Hoe

heads come in many different shapes and sizes. Make sure that the metal head is securely attached to the handle. A smooth wooden handle will resist splintering.

A **garden hose** carries water long distances. Attach two or more together to reach farther. Variable nozzles adjust to deliver everything from a gentle sprinkle to a hard stream. Brass parts and fittings are more durable than plastic.

Padded kneelers can help

to lessen the pressure on your knees. Kneeling is actually easier on your back than squatting. If both positions are too painful, bring a **stool** out to the garden to sit on or sit on the ground.

Rakes are purpose-built: The lawn rake is lightweight and used for raking up leaves and lawn clippings and for spreading mulch. Metal lawn rakes will last longer and perform better than plastic or wooden ones. The garden rake or ground rake has metal tines and is used for smoothing soil and clearing garden debris. Buy a rake that is securely attached to the handle. None of the parts should wiggle.

A **shovel** has a pointed, rounded blade and is useful for digging holes for trees and shrubs and moving soil. A **spade** has a straight-edge, flat blade and is good for digging straight-sided holes, cutting roots, and making edgings. When choosing a shovel or spade, the longer the handle, the more leverage you will have. Look for forged metal with a sharp blade edge.

A **trowel** is a mini-shovel used for digging small holes for planting. Look for a narrow, sturdy blade that will cut into the soil easily and has a comfortable grip.

A **watering can** is best suited for small watering jobs. It should have a capacity of at least 2 gallons but be easy to carry when full. Select a plastic or metal model with a removable spout.

A **wheelbarrow** or **yard cart** is used for hauling soil or leaves, collecting debris, and countless other tasks. The sturdiest wheelbarrows are made of one piece of heavy steel for heavy loads. A wheelbarrow is easier to maneuver than a two-wheel yard cart, but less stable.

TOOL CARE AND MAINTENANCE

Treat tools to a bit of TLC, and they should last for many years.

■ Always clean off any tools that come into contact with the soil before storing. Blast mud off with a jet of water from the hose or, if the dirt has hardened, soak metal parts first and then wipe clean with an old rag.

■ Digging tools and hoes need an occasional coating of oil (any vegetable-base oil will do) to prevent the blades or tines from rusting. Use a wire brush to remove any ingrained dirt or rust spots and then wipe clean with a rag. Use a clean cloth to apply the oil.

■ To sharpen digging tools and hoes, use a metal file on both the front and back edges of the blade, working at a shallow angle. Clamping the tool in a vise will make this easier. Finish by oiling the blade edges.

■ Wooden handles can be cleaned and then smoothed off with sandpaper or a sanding sponge. Polish with a natural, protective oil

such as teak oil.

■ After using pruning tools, remove any ingrained dirt or sap by using a wire brush or wire wool, if necessary. Wash the tools in soapy water and then dry them.

■ To sharpen pruners, loppers, and shears, hold the tool firmly in position and use a file, whetstone, or sharpening stone appropriate to the size of the blade to sharpen it. Sharpen only the cutting blade itself, working the stone in the same direction as the bevel. Two to five passes of the file or stone should be enough. Smaller blades may need to be worked in a circular motion. Next, tighten up any loose bolts on moving parts and inspect the tool to see whether there are any worn-out parts that need replacing. Finish by spraying with a tool lubricant. Don't forget to apply lubricant throughout the year, particularly after heavy periods of pruning.

DON'T GET A HOSING

Research has shown that numerous garden tools contain toxic substances, including hoses made with PVC. If you're using PVC hoses, you might want to . . .

• Minimize the hoses' exposure to direct sunlight. The heat of the Sun on water stored in the hose increases the amount of toxins leaching from it.

• Run the standing water out of the hose before watering food crops.

• Not drink from a hose.

• Avoid filling water bowls or troughs of pets or other animals.

• Avoid brass hose couplings, many of which contain unsafe levels of lead. Researchers suggest couplings of stainless steel, aluminum, or nickel instead.

ABOVEGROUND BEDS

WHAT A MAN NEEDS IN GARDENING
IS A CAST-IRON BACK, WITH A HINGE IN IT.
–Charles Dudley Warner, American editor (1829–1900)

Once you have decided where to grow your vegetables, consider how to do it: in the ground, in containers, or in aboveground beds. Here are some ideas for the last option. The other techniques follow.

THE RAISED BED

A raised garden bed is essentially a large plant container that sits on the ground. It is a box, built to your specifications, with no bottom or top, that is placed in a sunny spot and filled with good-quality soil.

A raised bed garden has many benefits. It . . .
- is ideal where ground soil is rocky, of poor quality, or abused
- is perfect for small spaces
- reduces weeds
- prevents water runoff
- provides a higher yield by enabling better drainage and deep rooting
- can eliminate bending or stretching to ground level
- gives you a longer growing season.

WOOD VS. CONCRETE

Raised beds are often made of wood. Pressure-treated wood (not CCA-treated) is certified as safe for gardening. However, the best option is cedar, which

HOW BIG A BED?

The amount of wood or concrete blocks needed depends on the size of your garden. Plants in a bed 4 feet wide will be easy to reach without requiring that you step on the soil. Length is less important; lengths of 8, 10, or 12 feet will provide plenty of growing area. In a raised bed, soil depth is important: Plan for a minimum of 6 inches of soil and know that 12 inches is recommended.

contains natural oils that prevent wood rot and increase durability. (Avoid railroad ties; these may be treated with creosote, which is toxic.)

Work with the lumberyard attendant to calculate the proper board feet to suit the desired size of your raised bed. While you are there, buy suitable nails.

Although concrete blocks are heavy to move, they are convenient: No stakes or nails are involved in making a bed with them. Concrete blocks are typically 16 inches long by 8 inches high and 8 inches wide. Calculate the number needed and consider stacking them two-high to create maximum soil depth. Be aware that concrete will increase the pH in the soil over time. After the first year, test the soil and amend accordingly. See page 34.

HOW TO PREPARE THE SITE

Before setting up the raised bed, loosen the soil that will

be under it with a garden spade or fork. Remove any grass. To improve rooting and drainage, remove and set aside 6 to 8 inches of soil. Then dig that depth again, leaving the loose soil in place. Add the top layer of soil to it and mix the layers together.

SOIL RECIPES FOR RAISED BEDS

More gardens fail or falter due to poor soil than because of almost anything else. Organic matter is essential, whether bought in bags or created by composting at home. Here are a couple of recipes. For each, simply mix the ingredients to combine.

For an 8x4-foot raised bed . . .
4 bags (2 cubic feet each) "new" (bagged) topsoil

How does your garden grow? Post a photo on 📘 @THEOLDFARMERSALMANAC

2 pails (3 cubic feet each) peat moss
2 bags (2 to 3 cubic feet each) compost or composted cow manure
2-inch layer of shredded leaves or herbicide- and fertilizer-free grass

For a bushel of soil mix . . .
1/3 bushel "new" (bagged) topsoil
1/3 bushel compost, peat moss, or well-rotted manure
1/3 bushel vermiculite or perlite
1/2 cup 5-10-5, 6-10-4, or similar fertilizer

Fill your raised bed to the recommended depth (at

least 6 inches, to 12 inches or more). If you built your bed with concrete blocks, fill the holes in the blocks with soil; they are containers, too, suitable for strawberries or flowers such as impatiens, petunias, or marigolds.

Now you are ready to plant seeds or seedlings.

GARDENING BY THE BALE

Straw bales serve two purposes: They are the plant containers as well as the growing medium. The decomposing straw inside the bale provides nutrients for plants throughout the growing season.

17

With proper preparation and care, strawberries, tomatoes, squashes, and other edibles will thrive in the straw. Carefully choose the bales' permanent location; wet ones are heavy and difficult to move.

The secret to a straw bale garden is to condition new bales for a period of 12 to 18 days before planting in them. Here's how to do it.

For each bale, you will need:
2¼ cups nitrogen-rich lawn fertilizer or 13½ cups balanced organic fertilizer (for Days 1 to 9)
buckets for water (optional)

1 cup of balanced (10-10-10) fertilizer or 3 cups organic fertilizer with phosphorus and potash (for Day 10)

Day 1: Set the bale on a porous surface, such as well-draining soil or a hard surface off which water will run easily. (The bale should not sit in a puddle.) Turn the bale so that the strings are parallel to the ground (this position provides the largest planting area). Sprinkle ½ cup of nitrogen-rich lawn fertilizer or 3 cups of balanced organic fertilizer evenly over the surface of the bale. Soak the bale thoroughly with warm water so that the fertilizer permeates the entire bale. To have warm water for the next soak, fill the buckets and set

---

A VOICE OF EXPERIENCE

My yard is on the side of a hill, with some very tiny areas that are only "sort of" flat. Small raised beds placed in the few level-ish areas have allowed me to have productive garden space without having to worry about my garden being washed down the hill during a heavy rain. In fact, I have managed to find appropriate places for six 4x4-foot raised beds. That is 96 square feet of garden space. My family, friends, and neighbors enjoy the vegetables from these small raised beds.

–*Marla, on Almanac.com*

them in the sun. Refill and repeat this step after every soak instead of using warm water from your tap.

Day 2: Soak the bale again, with warm water from the buckets, if using, until water runs out of the bottom.

Day 3: Sprinkle the bale with ½ cup of lawn fertilizer or 3 cups of organic fertilizer. Soak with warm water.

Day 4: Soak the bale with warm water again, until water runs out of the bottom.

Day 5: Sprinkle with ½ cup of lawn fertilizer or 3 cups of organic fertilizer again and soak with warm water.

Day 6: Soak with warm water again. You should smell and see signs of decomposition.

Days 7, 8, and 9: Apply ¼

USE STRAW NOT HAY BALES

When farmers harvest grains such as wheat, rye, or oats, they thresh, or shake, the grain seeds from the stalks, leaving behind dried stems. A baling machine gathers these stems into large round or small rectangular bales. These bales are true straw and the ones you want to use.

Hay bales are the entire grass stem, including grain seeds, which will sprout and grow when moistened. Hay is used as animal feed, usually. You want to avoid it.

cup of lawn fertilizer or 1½ cups of organic fertilizer to each bale daily. Follow with warm water. Most of the growing medium is created during these days.

Day 10: Sprinkle with 1 cup of balanced (10-10-10) fertilizer or 3 cups of organic fertilizer with phosphorus and potash. Soak with warm water.

Day 11: Moisten the bale with warm water.

Days 12 to 18: Set plants in the bale fed with lawn fertilizer.

Day 18: Set plants in the organically fertilized bale.

No other fertilizer is needed. Water the bale to keep the growing medium moist.

At the season's end, toss the remains of the bale onto your compost heap.

THE DIG LESS, MULCH MORE GARDENING TECHNIQUE

GARDENS ARE NOT MADE BY SITTING IN THE SHADE.
–Rudyard Kipling, English writer (1865–1936)

The practice of no-dig gardening—also called no-till, layer, and lasagna gardening—eliminates the job of turning over soil. Mulching replaces digging.

Mulch protects the soil surface from erosion, helps to maintain soil moisture, smothers weeds, adds fertility, and improves soil structure. Since there is no cultivation (soil turnover) involved, there are fewer weeds because new seeds are not brought to the surface to germinate. (Any weeds that manage to grow are easy to remove in the soft soil.) The key is to continually replace mulch as it breaks down into the soil.

The no-till method saves time and energy while preserving the overall soil structure. A no-till bed is essentially a compost heap and thus is rich in nutrients that make your vegetables strong and healthy—without the need for extra fertilizer.

No-till beds can be free-standing plots or raised beds.

CHOOSE A LOCATION

Identify the area for a no-till bed. It can be an existing bed, open soil, or even a patch of lawn. You will need to avoid stepping in the soil (to minimize soil compaction, which makes tilling even less necessary), so design your bed(s) with plenty of walking and kneeling space for easy access to your crops. Begin developing the bed at any time (fall is best) and allow several months to a year for the area to be suitable for planting.

Tools and Supplies

string
stakes
wheelbarrow
lawn mower or clippers
cardboard boxes (regular flat brown boxes without gloss or sheen, not corrugated or pizza boxes; no tape)
shredded bark
well-rotted or aged organic matter (compost or manure, leaf mold, wood chips, grass clippings, straw, and/or sawdust)

1. Mark out the beds. Make none more than 4 feet wide to avoid the need to step on the growing areas.

2. Clear the soil surface of any debris and rocks.

3. Mow grass short or cut weeds to the ground.

4. Add a 4-inch-thick layer of well-rotted organic matter.

5. Flatten and lay out cardboard over the entire bed area. Allow generous overlaps where you will have paths and cover with shredded bark or the like for a nonslip surface. The cardboard will kill all grass and weeds underneath.

ARE YOU A PLOT OR POT, INDOOR OR OUTDOOR GARDENER? GET IDEAS ON 📌 @ALMANAC

6. Spread a 1- to 2-inch layer of organic matter over the cardboard. Repeat layers of organic matter until the pile is 8 to 10 inches deep or, if you wish, continue to a depth of 2 to 3 feet; the pile of organic matter will shrink slowly over time.

7. Leave the new bed for several months to a year, or until the organic matter has compacted and composted into dark, rich soil. If the organic matter is still lumpy at planting time, start vegetable seedlings in plug trays or pots and transplant them when they've developed a sturdy root system.

8. An additional option: Top the compost with wood chips or other organic matter, such as straw. Add to a depth of about 2 inches; do not mix it into the existing compost. Push aside the wood chips to plant directly into the compost. This top layer helps to slow down evaporation and gradually feeds the soil below, reducing the need for additional fertilizers.

9. At the beginning of each ensuing growing season, spread a 1- to 2-inch layer of mulch or dead leaves over the bed. The mulch helps to prevent any remaining weeds from growing and keeps the soil cool and moist. After the harvest season, spread nondiseased expired/ing plants over the bed. They will add to the existing nutrients and help next year's crops.

21

CONTAINER GARDENING

WE MIGHT THINK THAT WE ARE NURTURING OUR GARDEN,
BUT OF COURSE IT'S OUR GARDEN THAT IS REALLY NURTURING US.
–Jenny Uglow, English writer (b. 1947)

No plot? Grab a pot! Lack of yard space is no reason not to grow something to eat.

When you garden in containers, you have more control over growing conditions, grow plants that are less susceptible to soilborne diseases and insect pests, and enjoy higher yields with a lot less work—which leaves more of the best part: picking the fruit of your labor at the peak of their perfection.

POT-TICULARS

Large plants need lots of space, and most roots need room to grow. Just as important, the bigger your container, the greater the number of plants you can grow in it.

Anything that holds soil can support a garden. Use barrels (a wooden half-barrel can yield an amazing amount of food), buckets, baskets, boxes, bath- and other tubs, and troughs. Just be sure that any container has drainage holes in the bottom.

Plastic pots won't dry out as fast as unglazed terra-cotta, and black pots absorb heat when they are sitting in the sun, which can also dry out the soil more quickly.

Building planters? Redwood and cedar are good, rot-resistant woods, although expensive. Pine is cheaper but will need to be lined with heavy-duty plastic to prevent decay. (Make drainage holes in the liner, too.)

Pots made of recycled wood fiber come in large sizes and are inexpensive and lightweight. Faux wood products made from recycled plastic last practically forever.

A VOICE OF EXPERIENCE

I have difficulty bending over or kneeling while tending raised beds, so I bought some used 35-gallon plastic barrels, removed the tops, drilled holes for drainage in the bottom, painted them brown to help to retain heat, and filled them with layers of garden soil and compost. Then I planted seeds and transplants for all types of vegetables. The result was a very prolific garden—I have 14 barrels now but plan on adding more—and no more bending or kneeling to tend my plants. Added benefits are very few weeds, which are really easy to remove, less water used, easy rotation gardening, easy-to-protect plants during cold or windy times, and more fun with much less effort to tend. Every year, at season's end, I top the barrels off with compost to replace any lost soil that seeps out of the bottom drain holes. These have been the best and easiest raised bed–style gardens that I ever have had. *–Douglas, on Almanac.com*

Hanging baskets make good use of extra space. Herbs, cherry tomatoes, or strawberries grown at eye level can be easily tended and harvested. A large window box can provide the makings for a fresh salad within arm's reach.

Whatever their size or type, place your containers where they are most convenient for you to care for and where the plants will grow best. Most vegetables need 6 to 8 hours of direct sun in order to thrive and produce well.

Place saucers underneath pots to catch runoff or rainwater and protect a deck or other surface. Remember to pour off standing water so that your plants don't drown.

A VOICE OF EXPERIENCE

In my early 20s, I moved into a small apartment building. Its roof, three stories above the ground, was a barren communal space. The idea of cultivating anything—especially food—on its surface was impossible to fathom. Never mind that there was no outdoor tap!

However, during 16 years there, I learned—through tragic failures and glorious successes—how to grow just about anything in containers: radishes in window boxes; herbs in a kiddie pool; small new potatoes in a garbage can; luscious strawberries, raspberries, and melons; diminutive hot peppers; and a monstrous tomato vine. I purchased some pots and dragged home others from the curbside economy. I saw potential in every receptacle. At times, the roof surface was so covered with planters that there remained only just enough space to do a delicate dance around it all.

–Gayla Trail, *Yougrowgirl.com*

If your sunshine is fleeting or you want to give the pots cover when bad weather threatens, consider placing your containers on a wheeled plant caddy. A two-wheel hand truck or four-wheel furniture dolly is another option.

Do not fill pots with soil from the garden: It is too heavy, can become waterlogged, and brings disease and insects with it. Instead, choose prepared potting mixes, aged compost, or a soilless mixture combined with organic matter.

To keep plants growing, feed them liquid seaweed, fish emulsion, or manure tea weekly.

Do not fill the bottom of a

FOR A SENSE OF SCALE . . .

• Lettuce and bush beans can grow in as little as 6 inches of soil.

• A large window box full of lettuce can yield a quart or more of greens per day.

• Mature tomatoes need a pot that is at least 20 inches in diameter and at least 12 inches of soil for their roots.

pot with pebbles unless the extra weight is needed to keep the pot from tipping over. It is better to allow as much soil and root-growing room in the pot as possible. Instead, cover the drainage holes with a piece of plastic screening to prevent clogging.

For proper growth, vegetables need consistently moist soil. Wind and warmth draw moisture from plant leaves, drying them out, so many plants must be watered as often as twice a day. Consider using self-watering containers, which have a water reservoir in the bottom to transfer water to the dry soil as needed.

To keep potted plants adequately cool and moist, double-pot them by placing a small pot inside a larger one and filling the space between them with sphagnum moss or crumpled newspaper. When watering the plant, also soak the filler between the pots. The moist filler acts as insulation.

HOW MANY PLANTS?

Plant lists are options; no pot below can support all of the vegetables in a list:
- 1-gallon pot: baby carrots, lettuce, or radishes
- 2-gallon pot: seven beets; six bush beans, if spaced 4 inches apart; one cabbage, chard, or pepper; baby carrots
- 5-gallon pot: two broccoli, one cucumber or melon, or long carrots (plant many and thin them out as they grow)
- 10-gallon pot: 24 beets; 15 peas or 15 pole beans, if spaced 6 inches apart; five chard; three cabbages or eggplants; two melons or squashes; one tomato plant; or long carrots

CONTAINER COMBOS

To maximize space and thus your harvest, plant root crops, low growers, and tall climbers together in the same container to best advantage:
- Mix quick-maturing plants, such as lettuce or radishes, with longer-growing ones, like tomatoes or broccoli.
- Group plants with similar needs for sun and water, such as pole beans, radishes, and

CONTAINER CAPACITIES

Potting mix is sold by volume. Most pots are described by their diameter. To translate pot size into amount of potting mix, use this quick reference.

Container size	Potting mix
8-inch	3 quarts
10-inch	1½ gallons
12-inch	2 gallons
14-inch	3 gallons
16-inch	5 gallons
20-inch	6 gallons
24-inch	7 gallons
30-inch	18 gallons
36-inch	24 gallons

Basic Potting Mix

2½ gallons peat moss
2½ gallons vermiculite or perlite
1¼ gallons screened compost or composted cow manure
2 cups fine sand (not beach sand)
2 cups time-release fertilizer pellets
½ cup lime (to counter the acid of the peat and keep the pH level near neutral)

Mix thoroughly. Makes about 6½ gallons.

lettuce; cucumbers, bush beans, and beets; tomatoes, basil, and onions; peas, carrots, and bok choy.
- For climbing varieties, put trellises, stakes, or other supports in place at planting time; stakes inserted into containers later in the season may injure the plant's roots. If a trellis becomes top-heavy, it may need to be attached to something other than the pot to prevent its tipping over. Position the container near a fence, wall, or deck railing for additional support.
- Think pretty as well as practical. For example, the vigorous vines of Italian heirloom 'Trionfo Violetto' pole beans are covered with dark green, purple-vein leaves, and their lavender flowers give rise to dark purple pods.

FINALLY, THE EASIEST-EVER CONTAINER GARDEN

Anyone can turn an ordinary bag of potting soil into a "grow bag": Lay the bag of soil flat. Poke a few drainage holes in the top surface. Roll the bag over. Cut a few holes in the new top surface. Insert seedling plants into the holes. Water and fertilize as you would a bed. For best results, set this sack into a wheelbarrow or child's wagon and move it into and out of the sunlight as needed.

A GARDEN STARTS WITH SOIL

ESSENTIALLY, ALL LIFE DEPENDS UPON THE SOIL. . . .
THERE CAN BE NO LIFE WITHOUT SOIL AND NO SOIL WITHOUT
LIFE; THEY HAVE EVOLVED TOGETHER.

–Charles E. Kellogg, soil scientist and chief of the USDA's Bureau of Chemistry and Soils (1902–80)

Good soil is the secret to a successful garden: It provides plants with the essential nutrients necessary to produce a bountiful and healthy harvest. Don't be fooled: Even though soil covers the ground, it is not the same quality everywhere, and there is no such thing as perfect soil.

Fortunately, the structure, texture, and/or nutrients in most soils can be improved. Here you will find advice and strategies for identifying the characteristics of your soil and properly amending it. Try one or a few.

KNOW BEFORE YOU GROW

The first step in assessing your soil is to test it. The results will reveal what it lacks and what to add. Soil that is lacking in nutrients or has a pH (acidity or alkalinity; see page 34) level that does not suit the vegetables that you

want to grow will cause them to underperform or even fail. Why risk it?

The Laboratory Soil Test

A lab test provides the most thorough analysis of your soil. It's best to have this test done at a laboratory close to where you live so that the recommendations that you receive make sense for your soil and climate. Most state Cooperative Extension services (usually located in or affiliated with colleges or universities) can help. Find

the service nearest you at Almanac.com/cooperative-extension-services.

A standard garden soil test costs around $20 and will measure your soil's pH level, nutrient content (calcium, magnesium, potassium, phosphorus, and sulfur), and percentage of organic matter (texture, or mineral components; more about that in a moment). The soil test report will be customized with suggested amendments to suit whatever you plan to grow—vegetables, flowers, lawn, or trees.

Soil continually changes, so have yours tested every 2 to 3 years. Keep records of test results, fertilizer applications, and any other soil amendments on pages 30 and 31.

The DIY Soil Test Kit

A do-it-yourself soil test kit generally reveals the

soil's pH level and nitrogen, phosphorus, and potassium content. The procedure is simple: You mix a small soil sample with water (usually a container is provided) and then add chemicals from the kit. These cause the soil sample to change color. A color match on a chart in the kit indicates your soil's pH level and nutrient content. Instructions for amending the soil condition are usually included. Basic DIY kits run from $10 to $25; more comprehensive versions can cost more. Kits are available at garden centers, hardware stores, and online.

The DIY Pantry pH Test

This procedure gives you a quick clue to your soil's pH:

- Place 2 tablespoons of soil in a bowl. Add ½ cup of vinegar. If the mixture fizzes, you have alkaline soil.
- Place 2 tablespoons of soil in a bowl. Moisten it with distilled water. Add ½ cup of baking soda. If the mixture fizzes, you have acidic soil.
- If your soil does not react to either test, it has a neutral pH.

The Earthworm Test

This test will indicate the tilth, or richness, of your soil. The best time to check for earthworms is in spring, when the soil's temperature has reached 50°F and its surface is moist. Using a shovel, dig up about 1 cubic foot of soil. Put the soil on a piece of cardboard, break it apart, and look for earthworms. If your soil is healthy, you'll find at least 10 earthworms. If your soil has fewer than 10 worms, add more organic matter to it.

AFTER THE SOIL TEST, THEN WHAT?

Lab soil test results note the presence of specific essential nutrients and provide recommendations

THE WEED TEST

Sometimes the plants that appear in your garden are themselves telltale signs of soil conditions. To establish the true quality of the soil, have a lab test done.

IF YOU HAVE . . .	YOUR SOIL IS . . .
bracken fern, dock, horsetail, nettle, Virginia creeper	acidic
broom sedge, burdock, horsetail, stinging nettle	calcium-deficient
cattail, horsetail, Joe Pye weed, marsh mallow	wet or poorly draining
common mullein, mugwort	infertile
crabgrass, field bindweed, plantain, quackgrass	hardpan or compacted
dead nettle, lamb's-quarter, pigweed, purslane	nutrient-rich
knapweed	nutrient-deficient
lamb's-quarter, wild mustard	alkaline
lamb's-quarter, ox-eye daisy, wild buckwheat	phosphorus-deficient

IF YOU HAVE . . .	YOUR SOIL HAS . . .
comfrey	nitrogen, potassium, and phosphorus
dandelions	iron, potassium, and phosphate
legume-type weeds, such as vetch and clover	nitrogen
nettle	iron and nitrogen
yarrow	iron and phosphate

for amending the soil to suit your purpose.

The Big Three

The primary nutrients are nitrogen, phosphorus, and potassium (N, P, K). These nutrients are available in chemical/synthetic (nonorganic) fertilizers (on the package, the number for each nutrient indicates the percentage of net weight contained within, e.g., 5-10-5) or as organic additives, as suggested here. For example, a 100-pound bag of 10-10-10 contains 10 pounds of each element. The rest is filler, which gives the fertilizer bulk and makes it easier to spread.

Nitrogen (N) promotes strong leaf and stem growth and dark green color, such as desired in broccoli, cabbage, lettuce and other greens, and herbs. (Most lawn fertilizers are high in nitrogen, with formulations like 24-4-12 or 20-2-6.) To increase available nitrogen, add aged manure to the soil or apply alfalfa meal (which also feeds soil organisms), fish meal (which is also an excellent source of potassium), or blood meal (which also repels deer). Note that nitrogen is released quickly, so wait until spring to add it to your soil. Be aware that proportions are not equal: 10 pounds of blood meal supplies the same amount of nitrogen as 10 to 20 bushels of manure, but blood meal does not provide the benefits of the organic matter in manure.

Phosphorus (P) promotes root and early plant growth, which help to anchor and strengthen plants, and it helps with setting blossoms and developing fruit, as well as seed formation. Phosphorus is important for cucumbers, peppers, squashes, tomatoes—any edible that develops after a flower has been pollinated. The most readily available sources of phosphorus are (fast-acting) bonemeal or (slow-release) rock phosphate, which also provides magnesium and trace minerals. Rock phosphate needs to be applied only every 3 to 4 years; however, tomatoes and root crops appreciate "snacks" of 5-10-10.

Potassium (K), also known as potash, regulates the flow of water in plant cells, promotes plant root vigor and disease and stress resistance, and enhances flavor. Plants deficient in potassium may display stunted leaves and fruit and be extra sensitive to drought. Potassium is vital for carrots, radishes, turnips, onions, and garlic. Add greensand (made from glauconite, an ocean mineral high in potassium and iron), wood ashes, gypsum, or kelp (dried, ground-up seaweed) to increase potassium. Kelp has the additional benefit of helping soil to hold moisture, thus reducing the effects of drought and frost. Because most soils already contain potassium, the third number in the fertilizer ratio tends to be the smallest.

The Little Three

Numerous trace minerals are needed for overall plant health as well, although in smaller quantities than those required by nitrogen, phosphorus, and potassium.

Calcium (Ca) improves general plant vigor and promotes the growth of young roots and shoots.

Magnesium (Mg) regulates plants' uptake of nutrients, aids seed formation, and contributes to the dark green color of leaves—important for effective photosynthesis.

Sulfur (S) helps a plant to maintain its dark green color and encourages vigorous plant growth.

The "Secret" Language of Soil Test Results

You are not alone if you are confused by the language on the lab soil test results. Here is an explanation of some commonly used organic soil amendments and the minerals that they contain, with the resulting effects.

Aragonite is a source of calcium found in mollusk shells. Since it is low in

magnesium, it is good to use if your soil needs calcium but does not need any extra magnesium. Too much magnesium can "tie up" other nutrients, making them unavailable for plants to use. If your pH is low, aragonite has almost as much sweetening power as limestone.

Azomite is a trademarked acronym for "A to Z of Minerals Including Trace Elements." Mined in Utah, it is ancient volcanic dust that merged with seawater 30 million years ago. It has over 60 minerals that are good for plant growth.

Bone char is burned bonemeal that provides a ready source of phosphorus.

Calphos colloidal phosphate is a good choice if your soil is low in calcium and phosphorus.

Dolomitic limestone will not only sweeten your soil better than pure limestone

LOOKING FOR GARDEN PLOT PLANS? FIND DOZENS OF IDEAS ON @ALMANAC

but also provide calcium and magnesium.

Granite meal is a rock powder that provides slow-release potassium and trace minerals without changing your soil's pH.

Greensand, aka glauconite, is high in potassium and iron and has small amounts of magnesium and other trace elements. It is good for loosening clay soils and improving sandy soil.

Gypsum is 23 percent calcium and 17 percent sulfur, so it provides calcium without raising pH levels. It helps to improve drainage by aerating the soil, neutralizes plant toxins, and removes sodium from the soil. The sulfur reacts

with water and forms a weak sulfuric acid that frees up calcium in the earth.

Hi-Cal lime is used to raise the pH and add calcium at the same time.

Sulfate of potash contains 51 percent potassium and 18 percent sulfur, along with trace amounts of calcium and magnesium. It is mined in the Great Salt Lake Desert in Utah.

Sul-Po-Mag, aka langbeinite, is used if magnesium and potassium are needed but more calcium is not. It does not raise pH.

Zeolites are found in volcanic ash. They can improve water and mineral retention in sandy soils.

Remember, there is no such thing as perfect soil. Do not try to master all of this information in your first year. Plant, observe, and then return here to see what works and figure out what to do next.

29

SOIL TESTS

DATE	RESULTS AND AMENDMENTS

SOIL TESTS

DATE	RESULTS AND AMENDMENTS

SOIL TEXTURE

SOILS ARE DEVELOPED; THEY ARE NOT MERELY AN ACCUMULATION
OF DEBRIS RESULTING FROM THE DECAY OF ROCK AND ORGANIC MATERIALS. . . .
IN OTHER WORDS, A SOIL IS AN ENTITY—AN OBJECT IN NATURE WHICH HAS
CHARACTERISTICS THAT DISTINGUISH IT FROM ALL OTHER OBJECTS IN NATURE.
–Charles Ernest "C. E." Millar and Lloyd Mildon "L. M." Turk, soil researchers, 1943

The texture of your soil is as important as its nutrient and pH levels. Soil texture—the amount of sand, silt, and clay, collectively known as mineral components—affects water and nutrient retention, air exchange, chemical reactions, and more. Each texture has value:

■ **Sand,** the largest particles, tends to be coarse-textured. Sandy soils have a gritty texture and drain quickly of both water and nutrients.

■ **Silt** consists of medium-size particles. Silt soils have a slightly slippery, silky feel. Silt soils retain moisture and nutrients longer than sand does.

■ **Clay** is composed of the smallest particles; it is fine-textured. Clay soils are heavy and smooth to the touch and can be rolled into a ball that holds together easily. Clay soils absorb moisture and drain slowly. As a result, they can become rock-hard in dry periods and waterlogged during wet spells. Clay soils are fertile, however.

A lab test known as a "textural classification" (usually for an additional fee at the time of a basic soil test) will reveal the percentage of each of these particles in your soil.

Loam, aka topsoil (more about this on the next page), is the ideal medium for growing most vegetables. It is a combination of soil mineral particles (sand, silt, and clay), organic matter (decayed plant matter), air, and water. These ingredients in combination result in soil that is fertile, free-draining, easy to work, and rich in organic matter.

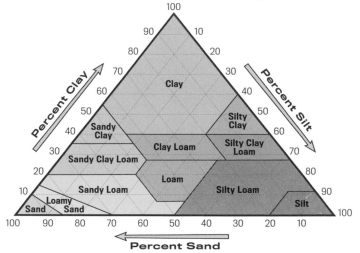

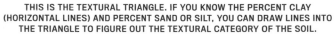

THIS IS THE TEXTURAL TRIANGLE. IF YOU KNOW THE PERCENT CLAY
(HORIZONTAL LINES) AND PERCENT SAND OR SILT, YOU CAN DRAW LINES INTO
THE TRIANGLE TO FIGURE OUT THE TEXTURAL CATEGORY OF THE SOIL.

SOIL FIXES

IF YOU HAVE THIS SOIL TEXTURE . . .	AMEND WITH THIS . . .
sandy	compost; humus; aged manure; sawdust with extra nitrogen; heavy, clay-rich soil
silt	coarse sand (not beach sand) or gravel and compost, or aged horse manure mixed with fresh straw
clay	coarse sand (not beach sand) and compost

TO IMPROVE YOUR SOIL, ADD THE PROPER AMENDMENT(S) . . .

bark, ground: made from various tree barks; improves soil structure

compost: an excellent conditioner

leaf mold: decomposed leaves, which add nutrients and structure to soil

lime: raises the pH of acidic soil and helps to loosen clay soil

manure: best if composted; never add fresh ("hot") manure; is a good conditioner

coarse sand (not beach sand): improves drainage in clay soil

topsoil: usually used with another amendment; replaces existing soil

THE UNDERSIDE OF TOPSOIL

Topsoil, aka loam, is exactly what it says it is: surface dirt. Depending on location, topsoil may be nonexistent to up to 12 inches deep. It is impossible to judge its quality by looking at it. State and local regulations of the quality for sale vary greatly (if they exist at all). If you plan to buy topsoil, take this advice.

■ **Ask gardeners to recommend suppliers.**

■ **Tell the supplier how you are going to use the soil.**

■ **Ask for test data.** If the topsoil hasn't been tested, ask for a small sample and have it tested yourself.

■ **Learn the soil pH and the soil texture classification.** A pH between 5.5 and 7.5 is acceptable. It's possible to raise or lower pH, but it takes work to change a soil's texture. Texture classification is based on the relative percentages of sand, silt, and clay particles in the soil (see opposite page); "loam" or "sandy loam" is best.

■ **Ask whether the soil has been screened.** Unscreened topsoil can be full of rocks and roots that you will have to rake out.

■ **Don't buy a product that has a chemical smell or other off-odor.** It could contain soils contaminated by petroleum or other potentially toxic waste products.

■ **Take home a sample of the topsoil** and sow a few seeds of different plants in it, if you have any concerns about herbicide residues. See how well the seeds germinate. Herbicide residues can affect some crops but not others. This process will also help you to determine whether the soil is infested with perennial weeds.

HOW TO TURN TOPSOIL INTO TIP-TOP SOIL

Any topsoil needs organic matter for holding moisture, improving soil structure, and retaining plant nutrients. Add plenty of organic matter to purchased topsoil, whatever its source, in the form of compost and composted animal manure.

Be sure to incorporate the new soil into the top few inches of your existing soil. This will promote plant root growth better than if you had simply spread it on top.

THE pH-ENOMENAL EFFECTS OF pH

To be a successful farmer, one must first know the nature of the soil.
–Oeconomicus, *by Xenophon, Greek philosopher (430–354 B.C.)*

Essentially, pH is a snapshot of the acidity (sourness) or alkalinity (sweetness) of the soil. It is measured on a scale of 0 to 14, with the low numbers representing the acidic levels and high numbers representing alkalinity. Soil levels usually range from about 4.5 to about 9.5. The number at the center of the range—7— is the neutral point.

Acidic, or sour, soil (below 7.0) is counteracted by applying finely ground limestone; alkaline, or sweet, soil (above 7.0) is treated with ground sulfur. A soil test will indicate your soil's pH and specify the amount of lime or sulfur that is needed to bring it up or down to the appropriate level.

A pH of 6.5 is just about right for most home gardens, since most plants thrive in the pH range of from 6.0 to 7.0, slightly acidic to neutral. There are exceptions: Potatoes prefer more acidity (4.8 to 6.5), and asparagus prefers more alkalinity (6.0 to 8.0). Refer to the list of common vegetables for each one's pH range.

SCIENTIFICALLY SPEAKING . . .

The letters p and H are a scientific notation: The p stands for "the power of" and the H represents the element hydrogen. The pH level refers to the concentration of two types of ions. The dominance of positive ions results in acidic soil. The dominance of negative ions results in alkaline soil.

THE pH PREFERENCES OF VEGETABLES

Asparagus	6.0–8.0
Bean	6.0–7.5
Beets	6.0–7.5
Broccoli	6.0–7.0
Brussels sprouts	6.0–7.5
Cabbage	6.0–7.5
Carrots	5.5–7.0
Cauliflower	5.5–7.5
Celery	5.8–7.0
Collards	6.5–7.5
Corn	5.5–7.0
Cucumbers	5.5–7.0
Edamame	6.0–6.5
Eggplant	6.0–7.0
Garlic	5.5–8.0
Kale	6.0–7.5
Kohlrabi	6.0–7.5
Leeks	6.0–8.0
Lettuce	6.0–7.0
Okra	6.0–7.0
Onions	6.0–7.0
Parsnips	6.5–6.8
Peas	6.0–7.5
Peppers, sweet/bell	5.5–7.0
Potatoes	4.8–6.5
Pumpkins	5.5–7.5
Radishes	6.0–7.0
Rutabaga	6.0–6.5
Spinach	6.0–7.5
Squash, crookneck	6.0–7.5
Squash, Hubbard	5.5–7.0
Sweet potatoes	5.5–6.5
Swiss chard	6.0–7.0
Tomatoes	5.5–7.5
Turnips	6.0–6.5

MY SOIL'S pH

DATE	TEST RESULTS/GOAL	AMENDMENTS

MAKE THE MOST OF COMPOST

*EARTH KNOWS NO DESOLATION. SHE SMELLS
REGENERATION IN THE MOIST BREATH OF DECAY.*
–George Meredith, British poet (1828–1909)

Consisting of decomposed plant material, compost is the gardener's best friend. Its ability to fix almost any soil problem has earned it the nicknames "black gold" and "the great equalizer."

Compost is also a soil conditioner that helps to stabilize pH levels in the soil. As organic matter, it attracts earthworms, which thrive in it, and their presence makes more nutrients available from deep in the soil.

Perhaps the best part of all: You can make compost yourself!

HOW TO MAKE HOT COMPOST

Many people think that composting is as simple as throwing all food and garden waste into a container and leaving it there for a couple of years. While you will indeed get compost that way, you can produce much better compost and get it much more quickly

if you follow these simple guidelines for hot compost.

Fancy compost bins are nice but not necessary. You can just pile up your ingredients on the ground. We recommend that the pile be at least 4 feet high, 4 feet wide, and 4 feet

long. Below a certain size, a pile will not heat up.

There are four ingredients needed for good hot compost: greens, browns, air, and moisture. The green and brown ingredients contain carbon and nitrogen. The ratio of carbon to nitrogen determines whether we label the ingredient a "green" or a "brown":

- **Greens** are ingredients with a relatively high nitrogen content (a carbon-to-nitrogen ratio of less than 30:1). Greens include grass clippings (which have not been sprayed with weed killer), vegetable waste, fruit peelings, annual weeds before they develop seeds, and old bedding plants. A word about grass clippings: Never add a lot all at once, as they will just form a slimy, matted layer. In fact, piling up loads of any greens will result only in a soggy, smelly mess.

- **Browns** are ingredients with a lower nitrogen content (a higher carbon-to-nitrogen ratio). Browns include straw; sawdust; wood materials, including chippings and shredded brown cardboard; and fallen leaves. Bedding from herbivorous pets, such as guinea pigs, is ideal, as their manure adds a bit of nitrogen into the mix.

Color is not always a reliable indicator of whether something is a green or brown material. For example, fresh grass clippings that are spread out and left to dry are still considered a green ingredient even though they have turned a brownish color; all that they've really lost is moisture. However, straw is always considered a brown because before it was cut, the main stems had died and much of the plant's nitrogen had gone into the seeds as protein.

- **Air** is vital to the process: Air is introduced when you turn or mix the compost; this speeds up decomposition.

THE SECRET TO SPEEDY DECAY

Both green and brown ingredients decompose much more quickly if you chop them up: Cut up kitchen scraps, shred woody materials, and tear up cardboard. This allows more surface area to be exposed to the microbes.

Ingredients should never be squashed down.

- **Water.** If you stockpile brown materials, water the pile to get things going when first mixing it. Build up the compost pile with layers of browns and greens and water where necessary to produce a moist (not soggy) mixture.

These four ingredients—greens, browns, air, and water—need to be balanced correctly for best results. Aim for 2 to 3 parts browns to

1 part greens, at least initially; more greens can be added as the compost "cooks." With air and moisture, you're giving the microbes that decompose the materials the best conditions in which to work. As they break down the organic matter, they give off heat; this, in turn, speeds up the decomposition. In a well-mixed heap, temperatures can easily reach over 150°F.

A good compost heap has a slightly sweet compost smell. If it smells sour or rotten, then it has too many greens or is too wet. In either case, the remedy is to mix in more brown materials to compensate.

If you follow this recipe, you should get a fine, crumbly-texture compost. Any remaining large pieces can be sieved, or screened, out and put into the next compost heap, leaving you with the very best food for your plants.

A VOICE OF EXPERIENCE

The first big vegetable garden that I planted struggled to survive. The soil was terrible—just gravel, with little topsoil and no organic matter. I didn't realize that my backyard was also the leach field for our septic system! We lived on a 250-acre farm and I could have chosen a much better location, but I thought that vegetable gardens belonged in the backyard. I learned the hard way that soil is essential to a successful garden—and it is much more important than what the neighbors think.

The next year, we plowed up a weedy side lot, and there I grew the best vegetables of my life in the deep, stone-free, sandy loam.

Now that I live on a rocky hillside and am not blessed with perfect soil, compost has become my best friend.

–*Robin Sweetser, gardener and frequent contributor to* The Old Farmer's Almanac

MY COMPOST PLANNER

DATE	INGREDIENTS ADDED	WATER ADDED	DURATION TURNED

MY COMPOST PLANNER

DATE	INGREDIENTS ADDED	WATER ADDED	DURATION TURNED

WHAT WILL YOU GROW?

BOTANY, N. THE SCIENCE OF VEGETABLES—THOSE THAT ARE
NOT GOOD TO EAT, AS WELL AS THOSE THAT ARE.
–The Devil's Dictionary, *by Ambrose Bierce, American writer (1842–1914)*

It happens to every gardener, especially beginners. You want to grow everything! Maybe you could, and maybe you should. Or maybe you should think again.

- Start by growing what you like to eat.
- Seriously think about how much time you have to devote to your garden.
- Understand the timing of harvest.
- And have a plan.

PLAN, PLAN, PLAN

Sketch your garden on the back of an envelope, keep each year's plan in a notebook, or use an app on an electronic device (more on that in a second), but plan your garden—and retain the notes; they will serve as a guide to effective crop rotation in future years.

Pencil and paper never go out of fashion, but an app adds a new dimension to the garden, whether it's in a plot or a pot. We realized the benefits years ago and now use and recommend

VOICES OF EXPERIENCE

Many beginning gardeners start out with good intentions, like these folks:

• Pat was determined to feed her family of six from her first garden. She was feeling so inspired that she had the whole backyard plowed up. Unfortunately, it was roughly the size of a football field! She was unable to cope with the vastness of the project: She could never look at the whole thing at once. It was too overwhelming!
The lesson: Start small.

• Chris planted a huge number of turnips. Only afterward did she learn that nobody in the family liked turnips. For months, she had to hide turnip in stews and casseroles so that the harvest wouldn't go to waste.
The lesson: Grow what you like to eat.

• Tom's garden was 200 feet long, and he planted it with beans in single-crop rows. Two hundred feet of beans is an awful lot of beans! He and his family picked what they could, invited the neighbors to help themselves, and still had beans left on the plants. To this day, his kids hate beans!
The lesson: Stagger plantings instead of sowing all at once.

The Old Farmer's Almanac Garden Planner as a companion program. It virtually guarantees your best garden ever, giving you help with planning your garden's size; knowing the number of plants that a space will bear successfully, specific companions, crop rotations, and sowing, planting, watering, and harvesting schedules; archiving your plans; journaling; learning via gardening tutorials; and a whole lot more—personalized to your zip or postal code. Learn more and try it free for seven days at Almanac.com/gardenplanner.

HEIRLOOM OR HYBRID?

Heirloom (aka standard or open-pollinated) varieties are "antiques." Many date

THE BEET GOES ON ... POST YOUR BEAUTIFUL BEETS AND TAG US ON @ THEOLDFARMERSALMANAC

from centuries ago. The term "hybrid" generally applies to varieties that have been bred since the late 1940s. Each type has value to a gardener.

Heirloom seeds vary little from generation to generation: The plant characteristics, the exceptional fruit taste, and the seeds are stable. Most heirloom seeds can be saved for starting new plants in the following year. The plants that heirloom seeds produce grow to be similar—although not identical—to the parent plant. (Occasionally, an open-pollinated seed will produce a "rogue" plant, one that differs

significantly from its parents. To avoid this risk, keep multiple varieties of any one vegetable at least 3 feet apart from each other.)

Hybrid plants result from the controlled crossbreeding of two genetically uniform varieties to produce seeds that will develop a first-generation (F1) plant. The new plants tend to be disease resistant, reach time to maturity reliably, and produce a predictable yield. However, hybrid seeds do not breed true: The plants may be dramatically different from the parent in, for example, yield and flower color, so their seeds are not worth saving.

Most gardeners grow both heirloom and hybrid plants. There is no right or wrong choice.

41

MY FAVORITE VEGGIES

YEAR PLANTED/VARIETY	SOURCE	HARVEST QUALITY

MY FAVORITE VEGGIES

YEAR PLANTED/VARIETY	SOURCE	HARVEST QUALITY

HOW TO START SEEDS

BEFORE THE SEED COMES THE THOUGHT OF BLOOM.
–E. B. (Elwyn Brooks) White, American writer (1899–1985)

Successfully starting seeds indoors is nothing of which to be afraid, but it does take some time and attention. Your goal is to have well-established but not lanky seedlings at planting time. Here's how to do it.

1. Make a list of what you would like to grow. To allow for good spacing between plants, imagine your garden to be one-quarter its actual size.

2. Purchase seeds from local retailers or catalogs. Consider teaming up with a neighbor to split a packet or an order. One seed packet often yields much more than one person or family will need, and seed companies sometimes offer deals/special rates for orders of a certain size.

3. Read the seed packet for the best time to plant. Then, estimate the time of the last predicted/average spring frost in your area: Consult the Frosts and Growing Seasons table on pages 12 or 13 or go to Almanac.com/frostdates

for frost dates specific to your zip or postal code. As a general rule, start seeds indoors no

SETTING SALAD VEGGIES?

• Cucumbers love temperatures of around 70°F and bottom heat. Put the pots on a heat mat or atop a refrigerator or water heater.

• Plant pepper seeds in threes: When the second (true) set of leaves emerges on the seedlings, remove the weakest plant in each pot. Later, transplant the pairs together and treat them as one plant in the garden. Their combined foliage helps to protect fruit from sunscald.

• Start tomato seeds in early April (in the Northeast and Midwest). Water only in the morning and keep the soil barely moist.

more than 6 to 7 weeks before the last spring frost.

PREPARE THE MEDIUM (SOIL)

The growing medium should be weed- and disease-free, absorbent, and fluffy.

■ Avoid garden soil; it is too heavy and contains weed seeds.

■ Avoid potting soil; it is too dense.

■ Consider peat moss pellets; they are simple to use. After being soaked, they expand and soften. Each one can later be planted with the seedling in it.

■ Or, purchase a bag of sterile seed-starting mixture and note the ingredients. If vermiculite, perlite, and crumbled sphagnum moss are not included, add them to help with drainage. (Some gardeners recommend using only these three ingredients in equal proportions!)

DIY Starter Soil

Want to make your own medium? You will need:

SHOW OFF YOUR SEEDLINGS! POST PICS OF THEIR
PROGRESS ON **f** @THEOLDFARMERSALMANAC

compost
coir (coconut fiber) or
    well-rotted leaf mold
perlite

Break up the compost or screen it, retaining the finely textured portion. If using coir, soak until it is fibrous and can be easily pulled apart. Combine and mix 2 parts compost, 2 parts coir (or leaf mold), 1 part perlite. Store in a covered container in a cool, dry place.

CONTAIN YOURSELF
Recycled containers—milk cartons, plastic or aluminum "take-out" trays, yogurt cups—work well, if they are clean and have drainage holes. Ideally, the containers should be 2 to 3 inches deep. Alternatively, use commercial trays or pots.

START THE SEEDS
Note any specific instructions on the seed packets. You may have to soak, scratch, or chill seeds before planting.

Start a few more seeds than you need or think you want. Assume that some of your seeds won't germinate or that they will inexplicably die off later. Plant a few extra, just in case.

Moisten the medium; it should be damp, not dripping. You can mist and mix it or try this: Put some medium into a plastic bag, add water, then knead the bag.

Gently but firmly, press the medium into the containers.

Carefully read the seed packet instructions (again).

Seedlings need space. Resist the temptation to sow thickly.

Sow large seeds in their own

containers. Place the seed on the medium, then sprinkle with dry medium two to three times the seed's thickness, or per the instructions on the seed packet. Press gently.

Instead of covering fine seeds, press them into the medium.

If you presoaked the medium, you should not need to water it. If not, water newly started seedlings carefully. A pitcher may let the water out too forcefully. A mist sprayer is gentle but can take a long time. Try using a meat-basting syringe, which will dispense the water effectively without causing too much soil disruption. In any case, use room-temperature water.

Label the containers. We all think that we'll remember which is which, but this never happens.

Cover the containers with a sheet of plastic (or a plastic bag) and put them in a place that is, ideally, consistently at about 70°F. Suitable places could be atop a refrigerator, behind a woodstove, in a sunny window, or under a light. Check them every day!

When you see a green sign of growth, remove the plastic. Transfer the container(s) to a slightly cooler place—one that is at about 60°F consistently—with increasingly more light, if the seedlings have been in darkness.

VEGETABLES BEST SOWN IN THE GROUND

It is not necessary to start these vegetables indoors, but some gardeners and nurseries do.

Beans, bush and pole
Beets
Carrots
Collards
Corn
Cucumbers
Endive
Kale
Kohlrabi
Mustard greens
Parsnips
Peas
Potatoes
Radishes
Rutabaga
Spinach
Squash, summer and winter
Swiss chard
Turnips

GOT LEFTOVER PACKETS FROM LAST SEASON?

Before you discard your leftovers, see whether the seeds are viable. Here's how:

Wet a couple of paper towels with warm water, wring out the excess water, and spread them in the bottom of a glass baking dish or on a plate. Taking careful note of each seed type on a separate piece of paper, lay the seeds in rows, five or 10 seeds to a row. Keep similar seeds separate, for example, tomatoes, peppers, and cabbages.

Spread a piece of plastic wrap over the pan or plate and seal it at the edges.

Taking care that the seeds do not roll, move the pan or plate to the top of the refrigerator. Check the towel occasionally; if the plastic comes unsealed, the towel may dry out. Mist it, if necessary.

In about a week, viable seeds should show signs of germination. The percent of the number that germinate should provide a clue to the germination rate of the remaining seeds in the packet.

LET THERE BE LIGHT

Many gardeners have great success starting seeds on windowsills, rotating them a quarter-turn every day, and monitoring moisture. However, this method has inherent challenges. One is not enough light, even in some south-facing windows. Cloudy days or a Sun that is low in the winter sky—leading to too much warmth in relation to the light that they receive—can cause seedlings to stretch and become spindly. To get more light on the leaves, try homemade reflectors: Place foil-wrapped cardboard or flat white–painted surfaces behind the plants.

Another option is to use fluorescent or LED (light-emitting diode) lights (see pages 199–200). Hang lights to be 4 inches above the containers during the entire growth process. (If you can not adjust the light's height, adjust the containers by putting books, pans, or the like under them.) Leave the lights on for 16 hours per day, ensuring a period of darkness. Maintain the room at about 60°F.

As seedlings develop, water less often and from the bottom. Allow the top half of the medium to dry between waterings.

Once germination has been achieved, you can start giving the seedlings some nutrients. Any all-purpose fertilizer solution will do, but be sure to mix at half strength and apply with a mister. Seeds contain enough nourishment for a seedling's early days, so when seeds are just starting, nutrients are not necessary.

OH, NO! WHERE DID MY SEEDLINGS GO?

Sometimes seedlings planted by even the most experienced and careful gardeners collapse and die. Often, the problem is "damping off," a disease caused by several fungi and fungus-like organisms and encouraged by poor drainage (too much moisture or dampness), little-to-no air circulation, and cool soil temperatures. To prevent . . .

■ Avoid overseeding and overwatering.

■ After setting seeds, cover the medium with 1/8 inch of milled sphagnum moss.

■ Mist seedlings occasionally with a fish or kelp (seaweed) solution.

■ Increase air circulation by putting a fan on its Low setting nearby.

OH, NO! NOT MILDEW!

The most common cause of mildew on soil is high humidity. Increase the air

"hardening off."

During the plants' last week indoors, withhold fertilizer and add water less often.

Seven to 10 days before transplanting into the garden, set the seedlings outdoors in dappled shade where they will be protected from the wind for a few hours each day. Gradually increase their exposure to full sun and windy conditions. This is the hardening-off period.

Keep the soil moist at all times during this period. Dry air and spring breezes can result in rapid transpiration.

After the hardening-off period, your seedlings are ready for transplanting. If possible, transplant on overcast days or in the early morning, when sunlight will not be too harsh. Here are a few tips:

■ Set transplants into loose, well-aerated soil. Such soil will capture and retain moisture, drain well, and allow easy penetration by seedling roots.

■ Soak the soil around new seedlings immediately after transplanting.

■ Spread mulch to reduce soil moisture loss and to control weeds.

circulation by lifting the lid (or whatever is covering your seedlings). See if you can scrape off the mildew without harming the seedlings.

To avoid this, be sure that your starting medium is viable, new/fresh, and soilless. The "lightness" of this material discourages humidity and encourages circulation.

HARDENING OFF

Before transplanting seedlings—homegrown or from a nursery—you need to prepare them for the outdoors. This step is called

BOOST THE ROOTS

Phosphorus promotes strong root development. To ensure the availability of it in the root zone of new transplants, mix 2 tablespoons of a 15-30-15 starter fertilizer into a gallon of water (1 tablespoon for vining crops such as cucumbers) and give each seedling a cup of the solution after transplanting.

MY SEED-STARTING RECORD

DATE PLANTED	SEED/VARIETY	MEDIUM	DAYS UNTIL TRANSPLANT

MY SEED-STARTING RECORD

DATE PLANTED	SEED/VARIETY	MEDIUM	DAYS UNTIL TRANSPLANT

MY SEED-STARTING RECORD

DATE PLANTED	SEED/VARIETY	MEDIUM	DAYS UNTIL TRANSPLANT

WHEN TO PLANT

GOOD SEASONS START WITH GOOD BEGINNINGS.
–*Sparky Anderson, baseball player, coach, and manager (1934–2010)*

There is no single day on which everyone everywhere can start planting; local and regional conditions vary greatly. But a few traditional beliefs and practices have proven favorable just about anywhere for centuries.

THE MUD CAKE PRINCIPLES
In spring, grab a handful of garden soil:

- If you can form it into a ball and it holds its shape, the soil is too wet for planting. It's likely that seeds planted in it will rot.
- Make a ball of soil and drop it. If it breaks into two clumps, it's still too wet for planting. If the ball crumbles, your garden is ready for seeds.
- If the soil sticks to your tools, it's too wet.
- If the soil crumbles through your fingers like chocolate cake, it's ready for planting.

As soon as the soil crumbles, give it a good stirring and let it sit for several days. Then top-dress it with compost or aged manure.

THE FOOTPRINT TEST
Step into the garden and then step back and look at the footprint in the soil.

- If it's shiny, then there's too much water near the soil surface to dig and plant.
- If it's dull, excess water has drained away and it's time to plant.

PLANTING BY THE MOON
For centuries, it has been common to link planting time to the phases of the Moon.

Tradition has it that crops that grow underground—root crops such as beets, carrots,

---

A VOICE OF EXPERIENCE

I just wait until I see the weeds starting to grow in my garden. Then I know it's time to plant hardy vegetables.
–*80-year-old farmer, on Almanac.com*

---

potatoes—should be sown during the dark, or waning, of the Moon, from the day after the Moon is full to the day before it is new again. The idea is that certain flowering plants need a period of total darkness to germinate and eventually bloom.

Crops that mature above the ground—e.g., cabbages, cucumbers, grains, leafy vegetables, parsley, peppers—should be planted during the light, or waxing, of the Moon, from the day the Moon is new to the day it is full. The belief is that the gravitational pull of the Moon raises groundwater similar to the way it does the ocean's tides, pulling nutrients from a plant's roots to its leaves and thus stimulating growth.

Many growers plant potatoes right after the full Moon and beans right after the change to the new Moon.

Does lunar gardening work? Many traditional gardeners, including generations of Almanac enthusiasts, hold that the Moon does indeed have an effect on plants. If you would like to try it, you can get the Moon phases for your zip or postal code at Almanac. com or see the "Planting by the Moon" chart in the annual print edition, with dates for planting specific crops in the given year.

PLANTING BY NATURE'S SIGNS

For just as many centuries, farmers also took their cues for spring planting times from observing what was happening in nature. The science of studying natural phenomena is called "phenology," and it makes sense: Trees, shrubs, and flowers—being sensitive to temperature and day length—

develop on a regular schedule based on local conditions. Other natural phenomena, such as bird migrations and the emergence of insects and amphibians (like spring peepers), also signify the coming of spring. It only makes sense to use these events as indicators of when the time is right for planting.

Here are some traditional observations that you could apply to your plantings:

■ Blooming crocuses are your cue to plant parsnips, radishes, and spinach.

■ Half-hardy vegetables, including beets, carrots, and chard, can be planted when daffodils blossom.

■ When the forsythia is in flower, plant lettuce, onion

sets, and peas.

■ Look for dandelions to bloom before planting potatoes.

■ When dandelions and/or wild violets bloom, plant bush beans; plant pole beans 2 weeks later.

■ When apple trees bloom, plant bush beans.

■ When the apple blossoms fall, plant pole beans and cucumbers.

■ When the quince is blossoming, transplant broccoli and cabbage.

■ When lilacs are in full bloom, plant squashes.

■ Transplant tomatoes when lily-of-the-valley is in full flower.

■ Transplant eggplants and peppers when irises are blooming.

See individual vegetable pages for more advice.

COMPANION PLANTS

IN THE END, THERE IS NO DESIRE SO DEEP AS THE SIMPLE DESIRE FOR COMPANIONSHIP.
–Henry Graham Greene, English writer (1904–91)

At the root of much garden folklore is the idea that some plants get along, while others antagonize each other. As with most folklore, many gardeners believe that this theory has a few grains of truth to it.

Plants compete for available resources, and some have evolved chemical defenses that discourage, or even eliminate, rivals. Little documentation exists to prove plant partnerships, but some have been verified.

Many herbs act as repellents, confusing insects with their strong odors that mask the scent of the host plants. Dill and basil protect tomatoes from hornworms, and sage reduces damage from imported cabbageworms. (Learn more about herbs on page 58.)With just about any garden plant, marigolds repel beetles, nematodes, and even animal pests.

Some companions act as trap plants, luring insects to themselves. Nasturtiums are so favored by aphids that the devastating insects will flock to them. Carrots, dill, parsley, and parsnips attract garden heroes—praying mantises, ladybugs, and spiders—that dine on insect pests.

Some companion plants are simply good neighbors. Lettuce, radishes, and other quick-growing plants sown between hills of melons or winter squash will mature and be harvested long before these vines need more legroom. Leafy greens like spinach and Swiss chard grown in the shadow of corn or sunflowers appreciate the dappled shade that these cast and, because their roots occupy different levels in the soil, do not compete for water and nutrients.

Plant foes—aka combatants or antagonists—have detrimental effects. For example, although white garlic and onions repel a plethora of pests and are companions to many plants, the growth of beans and peas is stunted in their presence. Potatoes and beans grow poorly in the company of sunflowers, and although cabbage and

> ### A VOICE OF EXPERIENCE
>
> I use basil sown with my tomatoes, as it invigorates the tomatoes and I can use it in pesto and other tomato dishes once it is harvested. Others, like chamomile with my brassicas, seem to attract good pollinators and are lovely sown between the plants. Beans seem to do a little better with summer savory, and cucumber appreciates a little oregano. Some of these are perennial and will come back next season, and all are useful in the kitchen or as potpourri. I use these in addition to flowers and have a useful, productive, and lovely garden.
>
> –*Sandra, on Almanac.com*

CROP	FRIENDS				FOES
Beans	Beets Broccoli Cabbage Carrots	Cauliflower Celery Corn Cucumbers	Eggplant Peas Potatoes Radishes	Savory (S.) Squash Strawberries Tomatoes	Garlic Onions Peppers Sunflowers
Cabbage	Beans Celery Cucumbers	Dill Kale Lettuce	Onions Potatoes Sage	Spinach Thyme	Broccoli Cauliflower Strawberries Tomatoes
Carrots	Beans Lettuce Onions	Parsley Peas	Radishes Rosemary	Sage Tomatoes	Anise Dill
Corn	Beans Cucumbers	Lettuce Melons	Peas Potatoes	Squash Sunflowers	Tomatoes
Cucumbers	Beans Cabbage	Cauliflower Corn	Lettuce Peas	Radishes Sunflowers	Aromatic herbs Melons Potatoes
Lettuce	Asparagus Beets Bruss. spr. Cabbage	Carrots Corn Cucumbers Eggplant	Onions Peas Potatoes Radishes	Spinach Strawberries Sunflowers Tomatoes	Broccoli
Onions	Beets Broccoli Cabbage	Carrots Lettuce	Peppers Potatoes	Spinach Tomatoes	Beans Peas Sage
Peppers	Basil Coriander	Onions	Spinach	Tomatoes	Beans Kohlrabi
Radishes	Basil Coriander	Onions	Spinach	Tomatoes	Hyssop Kohlrabi
Tomatoes	Asparagus Basil Beans Borage	Carrots Celery Dill Lettuce	Melons Onions Parsley Peppers	Radishes Spinach Thyme	Broccoli Brussels sprouts Cabbage Cauliflower Corn Kale Potatoes

SHOW OFF YOUR TRELLIS! POST YOUR CLIMBING VINES ON ⊙ AND TAG US @THEOLDFARMERSALMANAC

The beans pull nitrogen from the air and bring it to the soil for the benefit of all three. As the beans grow through the tangle of squash vines and wind their way up the cornstalks, they hold the sisters close together. The large leaves of the sprawling squash protect the threesome by creating living mulch that shades the soil, keeping it cool and moist and preventing weeds. The prickly squash leaves also deter raccoons, which don't like to step on them. Once harvested, the sisters provide a balanced diet from a single planting.

This trio is one of the easiest companion sets to grow. Try them in your garden:

In spring, prepare the soil by adding fish scraps or wood ash to increase fertility, if desired. When the danger of frost has passed, plant six kernels of corn 1 inch deep and about 10 inches apart in a circle about 2 feet in diameter. As the corn grows, mound up the soil around the base of the stalks until a hill about a foot high and 3 feet wide is formed. When the corn is about 5 inches tall, plant four bean seeds, evenly spaced, around each stalk. About a week later, plant six squash seeds, evenly spaced, around the perimeter of the mound.

See individual vegetable pages for more advice.

cauliflower are closely related, they don't like each other at all.

As you plan your garden, consider these plant friends and foes and take note. Record your plant combinations and the results from year to year and share it. Companionship is just as important for gardeners as it is for gardens.

CLASSIC COMPANIONS: THE THREE SISTERS

Do you know the legendary three sisters: corn, pole beans, and either pumpkins or squash? Native Americans grew these plants together long before Europeans arrived in the New World. In traditional lore, the plants were a gift from the gods, always to be grown together, eaten together, and celebrated together.

Each of the sisters contributes to the planting. As sisters often do, the corn offers the beans needed support.

MY PLANT COMPANIONS

CROP	COMPANION/S	EFFECT (IF NOTABLE)

HERB PARTNERS

I GROW MY OWN VEGETABLES AND HERBS.
I LIKE BEING ABLE TO TELL PEOPLE THAT THE LUNCH I'M
SERVING STARTED OUT AS A SEED IN MY YARD.
—Curtis Stone, Australian chef (b. 1975)

Even if you do not use herbs in cooking, most of these most common ones provide other benefits in the garden, such as by improving the growth and/or flavor of vegetables and/or deterring pests.

ANISE

ANISE
Pimpinella anisum
Annual
Anise and coriander, aka cilantro, enhance each other. Because of its long taproot,

SPRIGS OF ADVICE

Practice the three-plant theory when growing herbs: One for use, one for recovery, and one for starting new, either indoors or out.

If you have the room, plant herbs in rows, rather than in defined herb spaces, to reap serious quantities for the kitchen.

Planning to make pickles? Match your dill plants with your cucumber plants, one to one. Sow dill twice, 30 days apart.

Record plantings, quantities harvested, and rotations in this book—or note and save all of the information digitally on a desktop or laptop, with *The Old Farmer's Almanac* Garden Planner. Try it at Almanac.com/ gardenplanner.

licorice-flavor anise does not always transplant well; it is best sown where it is to grow, after the last spring frost. Plant seeds about ¼ of an inch deep in full sun in light, fertile, well-draining soil with a pH of 6.0. Thin seedlings to about 12 inches apart. Plants can become spindly, so provide shelter from wind, if possible. Beyond weed control and regular watering, it requires little care.

Harvest seeds by cutting ripe seed heads before they open and placing them in a paper bag to dry. Store the dried seeds in an airtight container away from heat and light. Gather fresh leaves as needed.

BASIL
Ocimum basilicum
Annual
Basil enhances peppers and tomatoes and repels asparagus beetles, flies, mosquitoes, thrips, and tomato hornworms.
There are many species and varieties of basil; this is the

BASIL

CHIVES

squash and repels imported cabbageworms and tomato hornworms.

Borage will grow in full to slightly filtered sun in slightly poor soil, in moist soil, or in light or sandy, well-drained soil with a pH of 6.6. Sow seeds in the ground or in a deep container; the plant grows from a single taproot to be 1 to 3 feet tall. It does not like to be transplanted. Thin to at least 12 inches apart.

Because borage spreads quickly, watch for flower heads going to seed and collect or destroy them before they self-sow.

Harvest flowers and young leaves as needed. (Note: Fresh leaves may cause contact dermatitis. Some herbalists warn that borage may be toxic to the liver.)

BORAGE

most popular for cooking. Start plants from seeds indoors in early spring. Transplant after last spring frost to warm (50°F), fertile, well-draining soil with midday full sun. Sow or thin to 12 inches apart to allow for air circulation and to prevent root rot. Basil likes heat and will droop in cool or cloudy weather. Water well at midday in dry weather.

Basil will yield continuously if pruned regularly. After seedlings have their first six leaves, prune to above the second pair. Later, prune the branches back to their first pair of leaves every time they get six or eight leaves on a branch. With regular picking, a dozen basil plants will yield 4 to 6 cups of leaves per week.

BORAGE
Borago officinalis
Annual or biennial
Borage enhances beans, strawberries, tomatoes, and

CHIVES
Allium schoenoprasum
Perennial
Chives enhance carrots and tomatoes, harm beans and peas, and repel aphids and Japanese beetles.

Chives can be started from seeds or by division. Sow seeds directly in fertile, moist soil in spring when the temperature is at least 65°F for germination. They can also be started earlier indoors. Chives grow best when they are planted at least 6 inches from other plants. Water well throughout spring and summer.

Harvest the flowers when they are fully open but before the color fades and cut chives back after flowering to encourage new leaf growth. Harvest the leaves to within 1 inch of the ground about four times a year. Every few years, lift the clumps of small bulbs, separate them into clumps of six to 10, and replant. You can let chives die back into the ground in winter or pot a clump and bring it indoors for forcing and using fresh all year.

CILANTRO, AKA CORIANDER
Coriandrum sativum
Annual
Cilantro/coriander enhances anise, harms fennel, and repels aphids, Colorado potato beetles, and spider mites.

CILANTRO

Cilantro refers to the leaf of this herb; the seeds are generally called coriander.

Cilantro is difficult to transplant; it grows from a taproot. Sow after danger of frost has passed or in fall in full sun in moderately rich, well-draining soil with a pH of 6.6. Set seeds ½ of an inch deep. Mulch seedlings when they emerge, then thin to about 6 inches apart. Sow seeds every 2 weeks for a continuous harvest. Water and fertilize sparingly, especially regarding nitrogen. Cilantro does not do well in damp or humid conditions.

Frequent cuttings of the leaves can extend the harvest, but eventually the plants will form flower heads. At this time, if you want a harvest of coriander seeds, stop cutting leaves. When the seed heads start to turn brown, cut whole stems, place them in a paper

bag, and hang it in a warm place. The seeds will drop off into the bag as the plant dries. When seeds are completely dry, store them in an airtight container away from heat and light.

DILL

DILL
Anethum graveolens
Annual or biennial
Dill enhances the cabbage family, lettuce, and onions,

SIMPLE STEM LAYERING

Mint, rosemary, sage, tarragon, and thyme are perennial herbs commonly propagated by layering.

To start a new plant with this technique, press a relatively long, low-growing stem toward the ground until it touches the soil. Lift or gently bend the tip of the stem so that several inches of it will remain exposed. Use a sharp knife to make a cut in (not through) the stem where it touches the soil. Sprinkle the cut with rooting powder. Then spread soil over the portion on the ground. (You can remove soil to make a shallow hole for the stem, if desired.) Secure the covered stem with a stake underground or a weight—brick or stone—above ground. Keep the area moist. In a few months, check to see if roots have formed. If they have, separate the stem from the parent plant, lift the new plant (keeping plenty of soil on the roots), and transplant it.

harms carrots, and repels cabbage loopers, imported cabbageworms, spider mites, and tomato hornworms. Plant seeds in early or midspring or start indoors. Transplant seedlings when air and soil temperatures have started to rise after danger of frost has passed and when the transplants are large enough to handle. Sow seeds and set plants in fertile, well-drained soil in full sun. Thin to, or set, plants 9 inches apart.

Dill grows quickly; if stressed, it will bolt and skip its leaf-producing stage, becoming leggy. It will also die out if the summer is hot, so to have a fresh supply of leaves throughout the season, plant successive crops every 3 to 4 weeks. Once established, dill does not like to be transplanted.

MARJORAM
Origanum majorana
Annual/tender perennial
Marjoram is a good companion for all vegetables and enhances sage.
Start sweet marjoram from seeds indoors in midspring by sprinkling them on the surface of a potting mix and pressing them down. Or start from cuttings. Set out seedlings after the last spring frost in a sunny spot with rich, well-drained soil. Thin to two plants every 8 inches or so. Keep plants weeded and

THE SYMBOLIC MEANINGS OF HERBS

Basil	good wishes, love
Chives	usefulness
Marjoram	joy, happiness
Mint	eternal refreshment
Oregano	substance
Parsley	festivity
Rosemary	remembrance
Sage	wisdom, immortality
Tarragon	lasting interest
Thyme	courage, strength

watered well until established, then reduce watering; marjoram is quite drought-tolerant.

Pick young leaves for the kitchen anytime. For drying purposes, gather a major harvest late in the season as soon as plants begin to flower.

MARJORAM

MINT
Mentha spp.
Perennial
Mint enhances cabbage, peas, and tomatoes and repels ants, aphids, cabbage loopers, flea beetles, imported cabbageworms, squash bugs, and whiteflies.

MINT

Peppermint does not produce viable seeds. Propagate it by cuttings (in summer), division (in fall), or layering anytime during the growing season. Cuttings root easily in water or moist potting soil. Plant seedlings about 1 foot apart in full sun to partial shade. Mint likes a good amount of moisture in rich, well-drained soil. Be aware that mint spreads rapidly underground by stems and runners. To restrain the roots and keep the plant manageable, sink a barrier into the soil around it when you plant.

Harvest young leaves as needed. Or, right before flowering, cut stems to the lowest pair of leaves.

OREGANO

OREGANO
Origanum spp.
Perennial
Oregano enhances pumpkins and repels pests in general.
Oregano can be grown from seeds if sown in late spring, when the danger of frost has passed. Watering is critical while the seeds emerge and when the seedlings are young; gradually taper off water until the soil is generally more dry than moist. Thin to, or set, plants 10 inches apart in well-drained dry soil in full sun. In spring or summer, you can take cuttings from the tips of new growth and transplant or divide clumps and replant.

Trim plants after they flower to prevent them from becoming straggly. In winter, cut back plants to within 2 inches of the soil and protect tender varieties.

Harvest leaves as needed.

BUTTERFLY MAGNETS
Dill

Marjoram

Oregano

Parsley

PARSLEY
Petroselinum crispum
Biennial usually grown as an annual
Parsley enhances asparagus and tomatoes and repels asparagus beetles and carrot rust flies.
Parsley is usually grown as an annual because it goes to seed in its second year. The two common varieties are the familiar curly-leaf and the Italian, or flat-leaf. Parsley does best in moderately rich soil, with a pH of 6.0. It can be a

PARSLEY

slow germinator and sporadic; for best results, soak seeds in water for 1 to 2 hours before sowing. Start seeds indoors 6 to 8 weeks before the last spring frost or, when the soil reaches 50°F, sow seeds ¼ of an inch deep where they are to grow. When transplanting, avoid disturbing the roots. Space plants 10 inches apart in full sun to partial shade and water well.

Once plants form good-size clumps, begin harvesting leaves as needed, cutting the outer stems first. Allow 2 to 3 weeks for regrowth between harvests. Pot up small plants and bring them in for winter. Six plants will easily provide enough fresh leaves for even the most ardent tabbouleh maker.

ROSEMARY
Rosmarinus officinalis
Tender evergreen perennial
In the garden, rosemary enhances beans, cabbage, carrots, and sage and repels cabbage loopers, carrot rust flies, Mexican bean beetles, slugs, and snails. In home closets, rosemary is said to ward off clothes moths and silverfish.
Rosemary can be grown from seeds: Provide bottom heat of 80° to 90°F. Do not overwater; acclimate it to the outdoors slowly. It can also be propagated from softwood cuttings of new growth or

by rooting branches that hang down. Plant it in well-draining, loamy soil, with a pH between 6.0 and 7.0, in a sheltered location that gets full sun. Allow 2 feet between plants. Trim after flowering to encourage leaf growth. Rosemary is hardy to Zone 8. Pot and bring indoors for the first winter and replant outdoors the next spring. In warm climates, second-year plants in a sheltered area will be frost-hardy. In cold climates, potted plants can be brought indoors each winter; established plants in a sheltered area with mulch can be left outdoors year-round.

Harvest up to a third of young stems and leaves at any one time, allowing the plant to replace its growth before taking more.

ROSEMARY

SAGE

SAGE

Salvia officinalis
Perennial shrub
Sage enhances cabbages, carrots, marjoram, strawberries, and tomatoes; repels flea beetles, cabbage root maggots, carrot rust flies, and imported cabbageworms; and harms onions and cucumbers.
Propagate sage in the spring by sowing seeds about ½ of an inch deep or by cuttings or crown divisions. During the growing season, you can increase plants by stem layering. Sage needs full sun and well-drained, sandy or loamy soil, with a pH of 5.6 to 7.8. Space plants about 20 inches apart in the garden. Water well until the plants are established; afterward, sage is drought-tolerant. Harvest leaves and flowering tops whenever you need them in the kitchen. When preserving leaves by drying, separate the leaves from the stems so that they dry more quickly. Prune sage severely in the spring and replace it every 3 years or so.

SUMMER SAVORY

Satureja hortensis
Annual
Summer savory enhances the flavor and growth of beans; it also benefits onions and melons and repels bean beetles.
Summer savory can be grown from seed; start indoors for best results. Set seeds on the starting soil and do not cover them, because they need light to germinate. Harden off seedlings before transplanting outdoors to well-draining soil (poor-quality soil is usually

SUMMER SAVORY

fine) in full sun. Plant them 6 inches apart in a spot that is sheltered from the wind.

Pick fresh leaves often to prevent the plant from becoming leggy; do not allow it to flower if you want to maintain its flavor. The leaves dry easily for storage. Summer savory dies with the first hard frost.

TARRAGON

TARRAGON, AKA FRENCH TARRAGON

Artemisia dracunculus var. *sativa*
Perennial
Tarragon enhances most vegetables.
When buying tarragon plants, make sure that they are French tarragon rather than Russian tarragon *(A. dracunculus)*, which is coarser and lacks

flavor. French tarragon tastes like anise, or licorice. Because French tarragon doesn't produce viable seeds (tarragon seeds for sale are of the Russian variety), propagate it vegetatively by division in spring, by layering in summer, or by cuttings in fall. Set plants about 2 feet apart in rich, well-draining soil and partial shade. To keep tarragon vigorous, divide the clump every 3 years or so.

Harvest leaves regularly during the growing season to make the plant bushier or gather a major harvest of whole branches late in the season. Handle the leaves gently to avoid bruising them. Prune all flowering stems to keep the plant productive. Mulch to protect against winter thawing and heaving.

THYME

Thymus spp.
Perennial
Thyme enhances eggplants, potatoes, and tomatoes and repels cabbage loopers, cabbage root maggots, corn earworms, imported cabbageworms, tomato hornworms, and whiteflies.
There are many species of thyme and much inconsistency in varietal names; if you want to maintain true plants, it is best to grow them from softwood

THYME

cuttings of new growth taken from existing plants or stem layerings. Common thyme *(T. vulgaris)* can be started from seeds indoors in early spring. Maintain a bottom heat of at least 60°F and water sparingly. In late spring or early summer, transplant cuttings or new seedlings outdoors about 9 inches apart in poor but well-draining soil in full sun. Protect plants from cold winds and wet winters: Take young plants indoors the first winter and plant them outdoors again in the following spring.

Thyme leaves and sprigs can be used fresh all year or dried. Trim the plants back after flowering to keep them from becoming woody and sprawling and to promote new growth.

HERBS IN MY GARDEN

VARIETY	PLANTING DATE	NOTES/USES

VEGETABLES

ASPARAGUS

ASPARAGUS INSPIRES GENTLE THOUGHTS.
–Charles Lamb, English writer (1775–1834)

Asparagus is one of the first plants to greet us in springtime! Doing best in regions with cool winters, it is normally grown from 1-year-old crowns but also can be grown from seed.

As a perennial, it will return year after year, although it may take 2 to 3 years to get started and produce. Once established, asparagus can be productive for up to 25 years with the proper care.

PLANTING

Plant asparagus in early spring as soon as the soil can be worked. Eliminate all weeds from the ground or raised bed. Dig a trench about 12 inches wide and 6 inches deep (8 inches deep in sandy soil and 4 inches in heavy soil) in rows 4 to 5 feet apart. Work in 2 to 4 inches of aged manure and/or compost. Soil should be well-draining; asparagus does not like its roots sitting in water.

Make a ridge of soil along the center of the trench. Spread a crown's roots to drape over the ridge, with buds pointing upward. Space crowns 12 to 18 inches apart. Fill the trench with soil and aged manure and/or compost. Cover with 4 to 6 inches of mulch.

Asparagus can be grown in a 15-gallon container, but under these circumstances it will not yield as much or live as long as it would as an in-ground crop.

To grow from seed, soak seeds in water for 24 hours. Plant in well-draining, wet compost, peat, or seed-starting soil in flats or peat cups. Harden off 12-inch-tall plants in a protected area for about a week. Transplant to a nursery bed after the last spring frost. In fall, note male versus berry-bearing female plants. In spring, transplant male crowns to a permanent bed. Remove female plants.

CARE

Water regularly.

Weed as needed (avoid tilling; it may damage the crowns) and re-cover with 3 to 4 inches of organic mulch such as straw.

If spring frost threatens, cover spears with 8 to 12 inches of straw. Frost can ruin a crop's quality and taste.

During the second and ensuing years, keep the bed thickly mulched; side-dress in spring and early fall. In late fall, cut down brown foliage to a few inches.

If necessary, transplant asparagus when plants are dormant, in early spring

RECOMMENDED VARIETIES

Female asparagus plants produce red berries on ferns; inside the berries are tiny seeds. Male plants expend no energy on berries, so they have stronger root systems and can be up to three times more productive.

For highest yields, plant male hybrids 'Jersey Giant', 'Jersey King', and 'Jersey Knight'.

Purple asparagus is bred to be that color when fresh; it turns green when cooked. Purple varieties tend to have thicker spears but fewer of them. 'Purple Passion' is tasty but is not an all-male variety.

White asparagus is green asparagus grown in the absence of sunlight to prevent the development of chlorophyll. White spears are slightly sweeter and less fibrous than green ones.

WIT & WISDOM

● *According to some taxonomists, asparagus is related to agave, hosta, and yucca.*
The small scales at the tip of a spear are leaves.
● *Dreaming of growing asparagus is a sign of good fortune.*

before growth starts or late fall before the first frost and after foliage is cut back. Dig and lift crowns with a garden fork; try not to disturb or break roots. Remove any weeds. Divide the clump carefully into two or more pieces. Water transplants. Do not harvest heavily in the following year.

DISEASES/PESTS *(see pages 158–166)*
Asparagus beetles; cutworms; Fusarium crown rot; rust, asparagus; slugs/snails

HARVEST
Skip the harvest in the first year. If possible, allow three growing seasons for crowns to become established. If you can not wait, harvest lightly in spring of the second year. Cut off 8-inch spears at or just below the soil line.

Plunge just-cut spears into cold water immediately to preserve their sugar content. Store spears in the refrigerator standing upright in water or wrap at the base with a damp towel. They will keep for up to 3 days.

Harvest young plants for 2 to 3 weeks and established plants for up to 8 weeks. Stop harvesting when the spears' diameter decreases to pencil-size or when a spear starts to open and form fernlike foliage. Let the spears grow, develop ferns, and replenish nutrients for next spring.

ASPARAGUS FERNS GATHERING STRENGTH
FOR THE NEXT GROWING SEASON

BEANS ARE EASY TO GROW, AND WHEN THEY BEGIN TO PRODUCE,
THEY ARRIVE NOT IN CONVENIENT INCREMENTS BUT IN A TIDAL WAVE.
–*Castle Freeman Jr.,* The Old Farmer's Almanac, *2010*

Pole and bush beans are commonly called "green beans." The main difference between them is their growing style: Bush beans tend to grow compactly, without support; they generally require less maintenance. Pole beans produce long vines that need to climb stakes or trellises; they typically yield more beans and are mostly disease resistant.

PLANTING

Beans are best grown in soil with normal fertility. If the soil needs improvement, add aged manure and/or compost in the fall prior to planting.

Beans grow best when direct-seeded. Sow anytime after the last spring frost or when soil is at 48°F, minimum. Too-cool soil can delay germination. Cover the soil with black plastic to warm, if necessary.

WIT & WISDOM

- *"Beans" often refers to something of little value: Something "not worth a hill of beans" is not worth much.*
- *To get rid of a wart, rub it with a bean and cast the bean over your shoulder without looking back.*

POLE BEANS REQUIRE A TRELLIS, TEPEE, OR OTHER TYPE OF SUPPORT SUCH AS A POLE (SHOWN) OR STRING.

ROSEMARY PLANTS WILL DETER MEXICAN BEAN BEETLES.

Sow bush beans 1 inch deep and 2 inches apart in rows 18 inches apart. Plant a little deeper in sandier soils—but not too deep. Seedlings can not push through soil that is too deep, heavy, dense, packed, and/or mulched; they will break their "necks" in trying to emerge. For continued harvests, sow every 2 weeks.

Before planting pole beans, set up a trellis, string, or other support. Try making a tepee: Tie three or four (or more) 7-foot-long bamboo poles or long, straight branches together at the top and splay the legs in a circle. Plant three or four seeds around each pole. As vines appear, train them to wind up the poles. For more stability, wrap string/wire around the poles about halfway up, encircling the tepee; this gives the vines something else to grab. Plant pole seeds 3 inches apart.

CARE
Once flowers appear, water regularly with about 2 inches per week.

Side-dress plants with mulch to retain moisture.

Weed and cultivate shallowly to avoid disturbing the roots.

If necessary, begin fertilizing after heavy bloom and the set of pods. Go lightly on high-nitrogen fertilizer, or you will get lush foliage and few beans.

Pinch out the tops of pole beans when they reach the top of the support to force them to put energy into producing more pods.

Use row covers in high heat; hot weather can cause blossoms to drop from plants, reducing the harvest.

DISEASES/PESTS *(see pages 158–166)*
Anthracnose; aphids; cucumber beetles; cutworms; Japanese beetles; leafhoppers; Mexican bean beetles; mildew, powdery; mosaic virus, bean common; root-knot nematodes; slugs/snails; stinkbugs; white mold; whiteflies; wireworms

HARVEST/STORAGE
Harvest beans in the morning, when their sugar level is highest. Look for firm, sizable pods whose seeds are not yet fully developed. Pick beans regularly while they're young and tender. If beans are bursting out of a casing/pod, they are overly developed. Snap (fresh beans should snap easily) or cut them from the plant. Avoid tearing plants.

Store fresh beans in an airtight container in the refrigerator for up to 4 days. Alternatively, blanch and freeze immediately after harvesting. Beans become tough over time, even when stored properly.

RECOMMENDED VARIETIES
The options are almost endless; here are a few.

Chinese (aka Asian) long beans (aka yardlong or asparagus beans): slender, 1- to 2-foot pods. Try 'Orient Wonder', 'Red Noodle', or 'Yardlong'. All pole.

French green beans (aka filet or haricots verts): thin, tender, 3- to 5-inch pods. Try 'Calima', 'Masai', or 'Maxibel'; in a container, plant 'Mascotte'. All bush.

Italian/Romano: wide, flat, 6- to 8-inch pods even in the hottest summers. Try 'Early Bush Italian', extra-large-pod 'Jumbo', or 'Roma II'. All bush.

Purple beans' raw 5- to 6-inch pods are deep purple and turn green when cooked. Try 'Amethyst', 'Royal Burgundy', or 'Velour'. All bush.

Snap (aka string or stringless): slender, 5- to 7-inch pods. Try 'Blue Lake 274' (bush), heirloom 'Kentucky Wonder' (bush or pole), or 'Provider' (bush).

Yellow wax beans: 5- to 7-inch pods have a milder flavor than green varieties. Try stringless 'Cherokee' (bush), classic 'Golden Wax' (bush), or 'Monte Gusto' (pole).

PEOPLE HATE [BEETS] BECAUSE THEY TASTE LIKE DIRT. ON THE OTHER HAND,
THERE ARE PEOPLE WHO EMBRACE THEM BECAUSE THEY TASTE LIKE DIRT,
AND I THINK THAT EATING DIRT OR SOIL, OR THE SMELL OF SOIL, IS PRIMAL.
–Irwin Goldman, beet breeder and professor of horticulture, University of Wisconsin

Beets are a cool-season crop that grows quickly in bright sun. They are a great choice for northern gardeners because they can survive frost and near-freezing temperatures. And did you know that beet greens have a delicious and distinctive flavor and hold even more nutrition than the roots?

PLANTING

Beets tolerate average to low soil fertility but not soil with a low pH. Before planting, test the soil's pH.

Note that in soil below 50°F, seeds will germinate in 2 to 3 weeks; in soil that is at least 50°F, germination takes place in 5 to 8 days. To improve germination, soak seeds in water for 24 hours before planting.

Set an early crop in March/April and a late crop anytime from June to September. Direct-sow ½ of an inch deep and 1 to 2 inches apart in rows 12 to 18 inches apart. Water and maintain moisture.

For a continuous harvest, make successive plantings about 20 days apart where temperatures do not exceed 75°F. Winter crops are possible in Zone 9 and warmer.

CARE

Each wrinkled beet seed is a cluster of two to four seeds. For best results, thin seedlings to 3 to 4 inches apart when tops are 4 to 5 inches tall, by pinching or cutting off leaves. Avoid pulling seedlings from the soil; this may disturb the nearby roots.

Weed regularly. Cultivate gently; beets have shallow roots.

Mulch, then water regularly with about 1 inch per week.

Avoid high-nitrogen fertilizer; it encourages top (leaf) growth, not roots.

DISEASES/PESTS *(see pages 158–166)*
Flea beetles; leaf miners; leaf spot, Cercospora; leafhoppers; mosaic virus, cucumber; wireworms

HARVEST/STORAGE

Harvest beet roots at maturity: 55 to 70 days, or when golf ball–size or larger; very large roots may be tough and woody.

Harvest beet greens at almost any time, beginning when thinning seedlings. Take one or two mature leaves per plant, until leaf blades are more than 6 inches tall and become tough. (Roots will not fully form without greens.)

Store fresh beets in the refrigerator for 5 to 7 days. To keep fresher longer, cut off greens, leaving a 1-inch stem. Store greens separately.

For long-term storage, brush soil from roots and bury in layers (but not touching) surrounded by dry sand, peat moss, or sawdust. Store in a cool, dry place (e.g., an unheated closet or basement). Sprouting is a sign of poor storage and leads to decay.

RECOMMENDED VARIETIES

Choose from many different varieties with different shapes and colors, from deep red to yellow, white, or striped.

'Chioggia': red skin; when sliced open, reveals red and white concentric rings

'Detroit Dark Red': round, red root

'Formanova': long, cylindrical beet; excellent for canning

For beets that do not "bleed," try a yellow variety such as 'Bolder' or 'Touchstone Gold' or a white one such as 'Avalanche' or Dutch heirloom 'Albino'.

BEETS' COUSINS ARE SPINACH AND SWISS CHARD; AVOID PLANTING BEETS WHERE THESE GREENS GREW IN THE PREVIOUS YEAR.

WIT & WISDOM

• *Beets have long been considered an aphrodisiac: Ancient Greeks thought that Aphrodite, their goddess of love, used them to enhance her appeal. Romans believed that beet juice brought on amorous feelings.*

BROCCOLI

WHEN KIDS LOOK AT BROCCOLI, THEY CALL IT 'LITTLE TREES' BECAUSE . . .
THEY SEE IT FOR WHAT IT LOOKS LIKE. WE, AS ADULTS, . . .
FORGET TO THINK FIGURATIVELY AND HAVE TO BE REMINDED.
–*Natasha Trethewey, American poet (b. 1966)*

Broccoli is a sun-loving, cool-season crop that can be grown in spring or fall. Excessive summer heat can cause bolting.

Because it is rich in vitamins and minerals and is a good source of vitamin A, potassium, folic acid, iron, calcium, and fiber, broccoli has been dubbed the "crown jewel of nutrition."

PLANTING

In early spring, before planting, mix aged manure and/or compost into the garden bed. The soil should drain well.

Start seeds in soil that is at least 40°F, in sun (so that plants do not get leggy), 2 to 3 weeks before the last spring frost date. Plant seeds ½ of an inch deep and 3 inches apart. Or set out four- or five-leaf transplants 2 to 3 weeks before the last

> **PLANT MARIGOLDS
> TO DETER IMPORTED
> CABBAGEWORMS.**

spring frost date, 12 to 20 inches apart, in holes slightly deeper than their container depth. Space rows 36 inches apart. (Close spacing yields smaller main heads but a higher yield of secondary heads.) Plants thrive outdoors in 65° to 70°F conditions.

For fall plantings (best in warm climates), direct-sow 85 to 100 days before the first fall frost, when soil and ambient temperatures are high. Or start seeds in late May.

Water well.

CARE
Spread low-nitrogen fertilizer 3 weeks after transplanting. (High-nitrogen fertilizer may cause hollow stems.)

Thin when plants reach 2 to 3 inches tall.

Water with 1 to 1½ inches per week. Avoid water on developing heads.

Mulch to reduce weeds and keep soil temperatures down. Avoid cultivation; roots are shallow.

Use row covers to minimize pests.

To promote the growth of a second head after the first has been harvested, maintain an active feeding and watering schedule.

If bottom, then top, leaves turn yellow, add blood meal.

DISEASES/PESTS *(see pages 158–166)*
Aphids; cabbage loopers; cabbage root maggots; cabbageworms, imported; clubroot; mildew, downy; stinkbugs; white rust; whiteflies

RECOMMENDED VARIETIES
'Calabrese': Italian heirloom; large head and prolific side shoots

'Flash': fast-growing, heat-resistant, disease-tolerant hybrid, with good side-shoot production; great for fall planting

'Green Goliath': heat-tolerant; giant heads and prolific side shoots

'Green Magic': heat-tolerant; freezes well

'Paragon': extra-long spears; excellent for freezing

HARVEST/STORAGE
Harvest in the morning, when head buds are firm and tight, and before heads flower. If yellow petals develop, harvest immediately. Make a slanted cut on the stalk about 5 to 8 inches below the main head, to allow water to slide away. (Water can pool and rot the center of a flat-cut stalk, ruining the secondary heads.)

Secondary heads/side shoots can appear for many weeks, if temperatures are not too hot.

Store broccoli in the refrigerator for up to 5 days. If it is washed before storing, dry thoroughly. Or blanch and freeze it for up to 1 year.

WIT & WISDOM
• *Originally, broccoli was eaten for its stems.*
• *Early Roman farmers referred to broccoli as "the five green fingers of Jupiter."*

BRUSSELS SPROUTS

Brussels sprouts are a member of the cabbage family and an excellent source of protein and vitamins. They have a long growing season and are generally more successful when grown for a fall harvest, as they increase in flavor after a light frost or two.

PLANTING

Start seeds indoors 6 to 8 weeks before the last spring frost.

Before outside planting, work several inches of aged manure and/or compost into the soil.

If direct-sowing seeds, plant ½ of an inch deep and 2 to 3 inches apart 4 months before the first fall frost.

Plant seedlings 12 to 24 inches apart.

Water well at time of planting/transplanting and with 1 to 1½ inches per week thereafter.

CARE

Water regularly to keep soil moist.

When seedlings are 6 inches tall, thin to 12 to 24 inches apart.

Fertilize with a nitrogen-rich product after thinning. Repeat every 3 to 4 weeks.

If plants appear to be in distress, drench with the micronutrient boron: Combine 1 tablespoon of borax with 1 gallon of water. (Avoid getting on bean, cucumber, peas, pumpkin, and squash beds, as boron can be harmful to these plants.)

Mulch to retain moisture, minimize weeds, and keep the soil cool.

Cultivate carefully, if at all; roots are

WE KIDS FEARED MANY THINGS IN THOSE DAYS—WEREWOLVES, DENTISTS, SUNDAY SCHOOL—BUT THEY ALL PALED IN COMPARISON WITH BRUSSELS SPROUTS.
–Dave Barry, American writer (b. 1947)

RECOMMENDED VARIETIES

'Churchill': early-maturing; adaptable to most climates

'Diablo': heavy producer

'Falstaff': red/purple hue that holds when cooked

'Jade Cross': high yield; compact plants

'Long Island Improved': heirloom; compact plants; prefers a cool summer

'Oliver': early-maturing; large, smooth sprouts

REMOVE YELLOWING LEAVES TO ALLOW MORE SUNLIGHT.

shallow and easily damaged.

Remove yellowing leaves to allow more sunlight on the stalk and focus plant energy on healthy growth.

To encourage plants to head up faster, cut off the top leaves 3 to 4 weeks before harvest. To harvest sprouts during winter, leave top leaves intact; they provide protection from snow. Cover plants with 10 to 12 inches of mulch.

DISEASES/PESTS *(see pages 158–166)*
Aphids; black rot; cabbage loopers; cabbage root maggots; cabbageworms, imported; clubroot; flea beetles; mildew, downy; stinkbugs; white mold

HARVEST/STORAGE
Sprouts mature from the bottom of the stalk upward. Harvest from the bottom when they reach about 1 inch in diameter.

If desired, after a moderate frost, remove all leaves, pull up the stalk—roots and all—and hang it upside down in a cool, dry basement, garage, or barn. Store stalks (no roots) for about 1 month in a root cellar or basement.

Wash sprouts only right before use, not before storing.

Store fresh-picked sprouts in a plastic bag for up to 5 days in the refrigerator.

WIT & WISDOM

- *Brussels sprouts are named for Brussels, Belgium, where they were first cultivated in the 16th century.*
- *In 2013, a team of scientists and schoolchildren lit an 8-foot-tall Christmas tree in London with the energy from 1,000 brussels sprouts (a total of about 62 volts).*

CABBAGE

CABBAGE: A FAMILIAR KITCHEN-GARDEN VEGETABLE ABOUT
AS LARGE AND WISE AS A MAN'S HEAD.
—Ambrose Bierce, American writer (1842–c. 1914)

Cabbage is a hardy, leafy vegetable full of vitamins, yet it can be difficult to grow; it likes only cool temperatures, and it can be a magnet for some types of garden pests. Rotating the cabbage crop can help to avoid a buildup of soilborne diseases.

However, by planning your growing season and providing diligent care, you may have two successful crops: one in spring and one in fall. Many varieties are available to suit both your growing conditions and your taste.

PLANTING

Cabbage is a heavy feeder; it quickly depletes the soil of required nutrients. Prepare the soil in advance by mixing in aged manure and/or compost. It should be well-draining: Roots that stand in water cause heads to split or rot.

Start seeds indoors ¼ of an inch deep

PLANT CABBAGE NEAR BEANS AND CUCUMBERS BUT NOT NEAR BROCCOLI, CAULIFLOWER, STRAWBERRIES, OR TOMATOES.

6 to 8 weeks before the last spring frost.

Harden off plants over a week. Transplant outdoors on a cloudy afternoon 2 to 3 weeks before the last spring frost date. Plant seedlings 12 to 24 inches apart in rows, depending on the size of head desired. (Closer spacing yields smaller heads.)

CARE

When seedlings are 5 inches tall, thin, if necessary, to leave the desired space between them. Transplant the thinned seedlings elsewhere.

Mulch thickly to retain moisture and regulate soil temperature. The optimum temperature for growth is 60° to 65°F. Young plants exposed to temperatures below 45°F for a period of time may bolt or form loose heads. Cover plants if cold weather is expected. Hot weather can also cause bolting.

Fertilize 2 weeks after transplanting with a balanced (10-10-10) formula. Three weeks later, add a nitrogen-rich fertilizer; cabbage needs nitrogen in the early stages.

Water with 2 inches per week.

DISEASES/PESTS *(see pages 158–166)*

Aphids; black rot; cabbage loopers; cabbage root maggots; cabbageworms, imported; clubroot; cutworms; flea beetles; mildew, downy; slugs/snails; stinkbugs; thrips, onion

HARVEST/STORAGE

Harvest when heads reach the desired

RECOMMENDED VARIETIES

Cabbages come in a range of sizes, shapes, and colors.

For Savoy types, try 'Alcosa', an early variety, or 'Wirosa', a late variety that overwinters as-is in southern gardens but needs protection in the North.

'Early Jersey Wakefield': heirloom; slightly pointed, 2- to 3-pound heads

'Gonzales': softball-size heads; good for small gardens

Quick-maturing 'Golden Acre' and 'Quick Start' yield 3-pound heads.

For an early harvest, try 'Primo' or 'Stonehead'.

For a fall harvest, try red or Chinese cabbage: 'Integro' and 'Ruby Perfection' (reds) and 'Li Ren Choy' (baby bok choy).

Disease-resistant varieties include 'Blue Vantage' and 'Cheers'.

WIT & WISDOM

● *A 127-pound cabbage won first prize at the Alaska State Fair in 2009.*

● *When boiling cabbage, drop walnuts (shell on) into the water; they will absorb the odor.*

size and are firm (mature heads left on the stem may split). Most early varieties will produce 1- to 3-pound heads.

Cut each head at its base with a sharp knife. Remove any yellow leaves (retain loose green leaves; they provide protection in storage) and immediately bring the head indoors or place it in shade. Alternatively, pull up the plant—roots and all—and hang it in a moist cellar that reaches near-freezing temperatures.

To get two crops, cut the head out of the plant, leaving the outer leaves and root. The plant will send up new heads; pinch off these until about four smaller heads remain. Harvest when they are tennis ball–size.

After harvesting, remove the stem and root from the soil to prevent disease. Compost healthy plants; destroy any with maggot infestation.

Wrap dry cabbage heads lightly in plastic and store in the refrigerator for up to 2 weeks or in a cool, dark place for up to 3 months.

TO HARVEST, CUT EACH HEAD AT ITS BASE WITH A SHARP KNIFE AND REMOVE ANY YELLOW LEAVES.

CARROTS

**THE DAY IS COMING WHEN A SINGLE CARROT
FRESHLY OBSERVED WILL SET OFF A REVOLUTION.**
–Paul Cézanne, French painter (1839–1906)

Carrots are a popular root vegetable that's easy to grow as long as it's planted in loose, sandy soil during the cooler periods of the growing season—spring and fall (carrots can tolerate frost).

Not all carrots are orange; varieties range in color from purple to white, and some are resistant to diseases and pests.

PLANTING

Carrots need loose soil. Till the soil, as needed, and remove stones, which can lead to a stunted and misshapen crop. Avoid manure and fertilizer, which can cause carrots to fork and grow little side roots; instead, work in old coffee grounds. If the soil is heavy clay or rocky, plant carrots in a raised bed at least 12 inches deep and filled with fluffy, rich, sandy soil (not clay or silt).

Sow seeds ¼ of an inch deep, 3 to 4 inches apart in rows 1 foot apart, 3 to 5 weeks before the last spring frost date. Cover with a layer of vermiculite or fine compost to prevent a crust from forming (which would hamper germination). For multiple harvests, sow seeds about every 3 weeks.

Carrots are slow to emerge, taking 3 or more weeks to show leaf. To help spot the first appearance of their tiny leaves, mix carrot seeds with quick-germinating radish seeds or sow radish seeds in rows between carrot rows.

Immediately lay row covers snugly over the soil to prevent carrot rust fly.

**CARROTS WILL THRIVE
IN FULL SUNLIGHT
OR PARTIAL SHADE.**

RECOMMENDED VARIETIES

'Bolero'; slightly tapered; 7 to 8 inches; resists most leaf pests and blights

'Danvers': heirloom; tapered; 6 to 8 inches; suited to heavy soil

'Little Finger': heirloom; 4 inches; good for containers

'Nantes': cylindrical; 6 to 7 inches; exceptionally sweet; crisp texture

'Thumbelina': heirloom; round; good for clumpy or clay soil and containers

For unusual color, try heirloom 'Red Cored Chantenay' and bright 'Solar Yellow'.

Lift only to weed, water, and harvest. If growing in containers, merely placing the containers off the ground will help to prevent the flies.

CARE

Mulch gently to retain moisture, speed germination, and block sunlight from hitting the roots directly.

When seedlings are 1 inch tall, thin to 3 to 4 inches apart: Snip the tops with scissors to prevent damage to the roots of the remaining plants.

Water with at least 1 inch per week to start, then 2 inches as roots mature.

Weed diligently.

Fertilize with a low-nitrogen but high-potassium and -phosphate fertilizer 5 to 6 weeks after sowing. (Note that excessive nitrogen in the soil promotes top, or foliage, growth—not roots.)

DISEASES/PESTS (see pages 158–166)

Black (Itersonilia) canker; carrot rust flies; flea beetles; root-knot nematodes; wireworms

HARVEST/STORAGE

Generally, the smaller the carrot, the better the taste. Harvest whenever desired maturity/size is reached—the size of your finger or at least ½ of an inch in diameter.

A frost encourages carrots to start storing energy—sugars; as a result, carrots taste much better after one or a few frosts. Following fall's first hard frost, cover carrot tops with an 18-inch layer of shredded leaves to preserve them.

To store fresh carrots, twist or cut off all but ½ inch of the tops, scrub off any dirt under cold water, and air-dry. Seal in plastic bags and refrigerate. Fresh carrots put directly into the refrigerator will go limp in a few hours. Carrots can also be stored in tubs of moist sand or dry sawdust in a cool, dry area.

Carrots are biennial. If you fail to harvest and leave the carrots in the ground, the tops will flower and produce seeds in the next year.

WIT & WISDOM

- *The Irish called carrots "underground honey," due to this root vegetable's sweetness.*
- *Carrots were the first vegetable to be canned commercially.*

CAULIFLOWER

CAULIFLOWER IS NOTHING BUT CABBAGE WITH A COLLEGE EDUCATION.
–Mark Twain, American writer (1835–1910)

Cauliflower is a sun-loving, cool-season crop and a descendant of wild cabbage. It is one of the most temperamental plants in the garden because it does not tolerate heat or cold. Cauliflower requires consistently cool temperatures in the 60°Fs, or it may prematurely "button"—form small, button-size heads   rather than form a single, large head.

It can be a challenge for beginner gardeners, but it may be a good autumn crop in many regions.

PLANTING
Before planting, mix aged manure and/or compost into the bed. Apply 5-10-10 fertilizer. Fertile soil aids in preventing buttoning.

We recommend buying cauliflower seedlings. Or start seeds 4 to 5 weeks before the last spring frost date. Set seeds in rows 3 to 6 inches apart and up to ½ of an inch deep. Water consistently during germination and growth.

Transplant seedlings 2 to 4 weeks before the last spring frost, setting plants 18 to 24 inches apart in rows 30 inches apart.

Be ready to protect plants from frost by covering them with old milk jugs, if necessary. Extreme cold can halt growth and/or form buttons.

Plant a fall crop 6 to 8 weeks before the first fall frost date but after daytime

PLANT DWARF ZINNIAS TO LURE LADYBUGS AND OTHER PREDATORS TO HELP PROTECT AGAINST APHIDS AND CABBAGEWORMS.

RECOMMENDED VARIETIES

'Graffiti': purple; tends to be milder and sweeter than white varieties

'Snowball': smooth, white, 6-inch heads

Orange varieties, such as 'Cheddar' and 'Flame Star', are creamier and sweeter than white varieties.

temperatures are regularly below 75°F. Shade plants from heat, if necessary.

Mulch to conserve moisture.

CARE

Cauliflower dislikes any interruption of its growth. Change, in the form of temperature, moisture, soil nutrition, or insects, can result in a premature head or the ruin of an existing one.

Water regularly with 2 inches per week.

Side-dress plants with a high-nitrogen fertilizer 3 to 4 weeks after transplanting.

When the curd (white head) is 2 to 3 inches in diameter, blanch it: Tie the leaves together over the head and secure with a rubber band, tape, or twine to keep light out (not necessary for self-blanching or colored varieties).

Brown heads indicate a boron deficiency in the soil. Drench with 1 tablespoon of borax in 1 gallon of water. (Avoid getting boron on bean, cucumber, peas, pumpkin, and squash beds, as it can be harmful to these plants.) Or provide liquid seaweed extract immediately; repeat every 2 weeks until symptoms disappear. In the future, add more compost to the soil.

For white varieties, pink heads can indicate too much sun exposure or temperature fluctuations. Purple hues can be due to stress or low soil fertility.

DISEASES/PESTS *(see pages 158–166)*

Aphids; black rot; cabbage loopers; cabbage root maggots; cabbageworms, imported; clubroot; mildew, downy; stinkbugs; thrips, onion; white rust

HARVEST/STORAGE

Plants are usually ready for harvest in about 50 to 100 days, or 7 to 12 days after blanching.

Harvest heads when they are compact, white, and firm. Cut off the head, with some leaves around it for protection. If heads are small but have started to open, harvest immediately; they will not improve. If a head appears coarse, discard it; it is past maturity.

Store heads in a plastic bag in the refrigerator for about 1 week.

For long-term storage, freeze it: Cut into 1-inch-size pieces. Blanch for 3 minutes in lightly salted water. Cool in an ice water bath for 3 minutes, drain, and package. Seal and freeze.

WIT & WISDOM

- *This vegetable's name comes from the Latin words* caulis, *for cabbage, and* floris, *for flower.*

- *The curd is the immature flower head; if left alone, it will form a seed stalk the next year.*

CELERY RAW,
DEVELOPS THE JAW.
–Ogden Nash, American poet (1902–71)

Homegrown celery is more flavorful than typical store-bought types. Celery is a long-season vegetable (130 to 140 days) and heavy feeder often grown as a winter crop in the South, a summer crop in the far North, and a fall crop in other areas. Transplants can be hard to find, so be prepared to start plants from seed.

Celery has three critical needs:
- cool weather; it will not tolerate high heat.
- constant water; stalks will be small, stringy, tough, and/or hollow if it goes without water.
- soil rich in organic matter and—because its roots are shallow (just a few inches deep)—fertilizer applied on top of the soil.

WIT & WISDOM

- *Through the centuries, celery has been thought to cure a headache, a hangover, a toothache, or arthritis and serve as an aphrodisiac.*
- *Nibbling on celery after a meal helps to clean your teeth and mouth.*
- *To crisp limp celery, soak it in cold water with a few slices of potato.*

CELERY THAT HAS GONE TO SEED IS BITTER AND TOUGH.

PLANTING

Before planting, mix aged manure and/or compost into the soil. Or work in some 5-10-10 fertilizer.

The need for a long growing season generally prohibits direct-sowing, but if desired: Set seeds ¼ of an inch deep. Thin to 12 inches apart when plants are about 6 inches tall.

To start plants indoors, soak seeds in warm water overnight to speed germination. For a spring crop, start seeds 10 to 12 weeks before the last frost date. (For a fall crop, start seeds in time to transplant seedlings 10 to 12 weeks before the first autumn frost.) Press soaked seeds into seed-starting soil; do not cover with soil. Cover starter trays/pots with plastic wrap to retain moisture. Germination should occur in about a week.

Soon after seedlings appear, place a fluorescent grow light 3 inches above them for 16 hours a day (plants need dark, too). Maintain an ambient temperature of 70° to 75°F during the day and 60° to 65°F at night.

Mist regularly.

When seedings are 2 inches tall, transplant them to individual peat pots or to deeper flats with new potting soil. In flats, set plants at least 2 inches apart.

Harden off seedlings before transplanting by reducing water slightly and putting them outdoors for a couple of hours each day.

Transplant celery when the soil temperature is at least 50°F and nighttime temperatures do not dip below 40°F. (Cold weather after planting can cause bolting.)

Plant seedlings 8 to 10 inches apart. Water thoroughly.

RECOMMENDED VARIETIES

'Afina': quick-growing; hardy; slender, dark green stalks up to 30 inches

'Conquistador': tolerant of heat, water shortages, and average soil fertility

'Golden Self Blanching': heirloom dwarf; stringless stalks; good for small gardens

'Utah 52-70R Improved': compact; matures at 18 inches tall; disease-resistant

CARE

Water regularly with 2 inches per week and more in hot, dry weather.

Use row covers for the first 4 to 5 weeks to control pests.

When plants are 6 inches tall, mulch to keep the soil moist and the roots cool.

Side-dress with compost.

In the second and third months, side-dress with 1 tablespoon of 5-10-10 fertilizer 3 to 4 inches from each plant.

half-gallon milk cartons (cut out tops and bottoms), or the like. Do not cover celery leaves.

Seeds are mature when they dry on the plant and fall off at the slightest touch.

DISEASES/PESTS *(see pages 158–166)*

Carrot rust flies; earwigs, European; flea beetles; mosaic virus, cucumber; slugs/snails

DARK GREEN STALKS ARE TOUGHER BUT CONTAIN MORE NUTRIENTS THAN PALE ONES.

Cover with soil.

Weed carefully; celery roots are shallow and easily disturbed.

Tie growing stalks together to keep them from sprawling.

Blanch (wrap or cover) stalks to eliminate any bitter taste and produce pale green stalks. Use anything that will keep out light: brown-bag paper or cardboard (secure with old nylon stockings, string, vegetable wires),

HARVEST/STORAGE

Harvest outer stalks at 8 inches tall. Dark green stalks are tougher but contain more nutrients than pale ones.

Keep celery in the ground for up to 1 month by building up soil around it to maintain an ideal temperature. It will tolerate a light frost but not consecutive frosts.

Store celery in a plastic bag in the refrigerator for several weeks.

I KNOW MY CORN PLANTS INTIMATELY, AND I FIND
IT A GREAT PLEASURE TO KNOW THEM.
*—Barbara McClintock, American corn chromosome research scientist
and Nobel Prize winner (1902–92)*

Sweet corn is an annual crop that requires a long, frost-free growing season. Early, mid-, and late-season varieties extend the harvest. Past optimal harvest time, corn loses its flavor quickly, as sugars convert to starch.

PLANTING

In the fall prior to planting, work aged manure and/or compost into the bed. The soil should be well-draining yet consistently moist.

Starting corn seeds indoors is not generally recommended.

Plan for sufficient pollination: Plant blocks of at least four rows. Or, for example, in a 10x10-foot plot, lay a drip line in ever-increasing circles spaced 1 foot apart and plant a seed at each emitter.

To speed germination, moisten seeds, wrap in moist paper towels, and store in a plastic bag for 24 hours. Sow seeds 1½ to 2 inches deep and 4 to 6 inches apart in rows 30 to 36 inches apart

2 weeks after the last spring frost, if the soil is above 60°F. Super-sweet varieties prefer 65°F soil. In cold zones, cover the ground with black plastic to prewarm it and cut holes in it to plant seeds. The optimum temperature for all sweet corn is 65° to 85°F.

Apply a 10-10-10 fertilizer at planting time or skip it if you are confident that the soil is adequately rich.

Water well.

CARE

When plants are 3 to 4 inches tall, thin to 8 to 12 inches apart.

Side-dress plants with a high-nitrogen fertilizer when corn is 8 inches tall. Repeat when it is knee high (18 inches).

Weed carefully to avoid damaging corn's shallow roots.

To keep stalks standing straight during high winds, mound soil around the base of 12-inch-tall plants.

Water regularly with 2 inches per week. Mulch to reduce evaporation.

Tillers, or suckers, are secondary shoots that may develop low on the stalk later in season. They do not adversely affect the main stalk.

DISEASES/PESTS *(see pages 158–166)*

Anthracnose; corn earworms; cucumber beetles, spotted (southern corn rootworm); cutworms; earwigs, European; flea beetles; Japanese beetles; mildew, downy; wireworms

HARVEST/STORAGE

The warmer the air, the more quickly corn matures. It is usually ripe about 15 to 23 days after silking and sooner if temperatures are exceptionally high.

When two ears grow on a stalk, the upper ear matures 1 to 2 days before the lower one.

At harvest, ears should be rounded

RECOMMENDED VARIETIES

Sweet corn can be normal, sugar-enhanced, or supersweet. Each type contains a different level of sucrose, changing the corn's flavor and texture. Sweeter varieties stay sweeter longer. For best flavor, plant only one variety.

'Argent': sugar-enhanced variety; good taste; white kernels

'Iochief': midseason, normal-sugar variety; yellow kernels

'Luther Hill': dwarf; normal-sugar variety; 4- to 6-inch ears on 4- to 5-foot stalks; white kernels. Grow at least nine dwarf plants in a block of three or four rows.

'Silver Queen': normal-sugar variety; resistant to some bacterial diseases; white kernels

'Sweet Sunshine': supersweet variety; disease-resistant; high yield; yellow kernels

WIT & WISDOM

• Corn planted under a waning Moon grows more slowly but yields bigger ears.

• A cornstalk grows slowly until it reaches about 24 inches;
then it grows 3 to 4 inches per day in hot weather.

• If your corn shucks harder than usual, prepare for a cold winter.

AT HARVEST, EARS SHOULD BE ROUNDED, NOT POINTED, AND TASSELS SHOULD BE BROWN.

or blunt, not pointed, with tassels turning brown and kernels full and milky. To test, pull down some husk and pierce a kernel with a fingernail. If it's white, or milky, it's ready. The milk stage is brief; in hot weather (over 85°F), sweet corn is at peak for only 1 to 2 days, so check it frequently. Corn harvested a few days after milk stage will not be as sweet.

Pull an ear downward, then twist to remove from a stalk.

If immature corn suffers a late-season frost, the plants and cobs can be damaged and result in the death of the plant or poor-tasting corn.

Prepare corn for use immediately after picking. Sweet corn freezes well. Blanch cobs, then remove kernels and package, seal, and freeze.

BECAUSE IT IS WIND-POLLINATED, CORN SHOULD BE PLANTED IN BLOCKS, NOT SINGLE ROWS.

CUCUMBERS

An easy-care vegetable, cucumbers grow quickly when they receive full sun and plenty of water. Most varieties thrive in any amount of space, thanks to the plant's ability to climb. Of course, these prolific veggies are perfect for pickling!

There are two types of cucumber plants:

- **Vining cucumbers,** the most common varieties, grow on vigorous vines up a trellis or fence, shaded by large leaves. Providing support results in clean (vs. those that grow atop soil), often abundant, and easy-to-pick cucumbers.

- **Bush cucumbers** are nicely suited to containers and small gardens.

Make successive plantings (every 2 weeks) for continued harvests. In warm soil, cucumbers will grow quickly and ripen in about 6 weeks.

PLANTING

Prior to planting, add 2 inches of aged manure and/or compost to the bed and work it in to a depth of 6 to 8 inches. Soil should be moist but well-draining (not soggy) and warm.

For an early crop, start cucumber seeds indoors about 3 weeks before transplant time. Provide bottom heat of about 70°F with a heating pad or place seed flats on top of a refrigerator or water heater.

Cucumber seeds require soil to be at least 70°F for germination; seedlings set best at that temperature, too. (In cooler

HEAVEN IS A HOMEGROWN
CUCUMBER.
*—Alys Fowler, English journalist and
gardener (b. 1978)*

RECOMMENDED VARIETIES

'Boston Pickling': vine; heirloom; bred for pickling

'Burpless Bush Hybrid': bush; good for small gardens, pots, or pickling

'Bush Crop': bush; dwarf plants; high yield; good for eating fresh

'Calypso': vine; high yield; disease-resistant; perfect picklers

'Lemon': vine; round; yellow; supersweet; fun for kids

'Parisian Pickling': vine; long and thin; good for gherkins or cornichons

'Sweet Success': vine; good for greenhouse growing; requires no pollinators; seedless

climates, warm the soil by covering it with black plastic.) Plant outside no earlier than 2 weeks before the last spring frost. Cucumbers are extremely susceptible to frost damage.

Sow seeds 1 inch deep and about 3 to 5 feet apart, depending on variety. For vines trained on a trellis, space seeds or plants 1 foot apart. If desired, apply a 5-10-10 liquid fertilizer.

When seedlings emerge, begin to water frequently.

Mulch seedlings with pine straw, chopped leaves, or other organic mulch to deter weeds and pests and to keep bush cucumbers off the ground to avoid disease.

CARE

Cucumbers require consistent watering—1 inch per week and more in high heat. Water slowly in mornings or early afternoons. Avoid wetting leaves; leaf diseases (e.g., powdery mildew) can ruin the plant. If possible, water your cucumbers with a soaker hose or drip irrigation to keep the foliage dry.

Mulch to retain moisture.

Use row covers or berry baskets if pests appear.

When seedlings are 4 inches tall, thin to be 1½ feet apart.

Side-dress plants with aged manure

INCONSISTENT WATERING LEADS TO BITTER-TASTING CUCUMBERS.

WIT & WISDOM

• *"Burpless" cucumbers have little to no cucurbitacin, which causes bitterness and increases the likelihood of burping by those who consume it.*

• *Purée cucumbers in the blender to make a great facial for toning the skin. The cukes clarify the skin and reduce puffiness.*

and/or compost.

Starting 1 week after flowers bloom and continuing every 3 weeks thereafter, apply a 5-10-10 liquid fertilizer directly to the soil. Or work a granular fertilizer into the soil. Note that overfertilizing can result in stunted fruit.

Spray vines with sugar water to attract bees and set more fruit.

Lack of fruit may be due to poor pollination, rain, cold, disease, or insecticides. The first flowers are all male. For pollination, both female and male flowers must be blooming at the same time. (Female flowers have a small, cucumber-shape swelling at the base; this will become the fruit.) If necessary, try hand pollination: Dip a cotton swab into the male flower's pollen and transfer it to the center of the female flower.

Curling (aka crooking) can be due to pollination problems (e.g., too few pollinators or heat-damaged pollen); lack of nutrients, water, light, or heat; or pests and diseases.

DISEASES/PESTS *(see pages 158–166)*
Anthracnose; aphids; blossom-end rot; cucumber beetles; mildew, downy; mildew, powdery; mosaic virus, cucumber; squash bugs; whiteflies

HARVEST/STORAGE
Cucumbers grow quickly: Pick every couple of days. Failure to pick can result in lower plant productivity.

A cucumber is of highest quality when it is uniformly green, firm, and crisp. Use a knife or clippers to cut the stem above the fruit. Pulling the fruit may damage the vine.

CURLING CAN BE DUE TO POLLINATION PROBLEMS; LACK OF NUTRIENTS, WATER, LIGHT, OR HEAT; OR PESTS AND DISEASES.

Harvest slicing cucumbers at 6 to 8 inches in length, dill picklers at 4 to 6 inches, and other pickling cukes at 2 inches. Burpless fruit, grown for their mild flavor and thin skin, can be up to 10 inches, or even longer.

Cucumbers left on the vine too long will have tough skin, hard seeds, and a bitter taste.

To store, wrap tightly in plastic wrap and keep in the refrigerator for 7 to 10 days.

EDAMAME

IT'S LIKE GREEN POPCORN, IN A WAY. IT HAS THE
SAME COMPULSIVE QUALITY—[IT IS] REALLY GREAT FINGER FOOD.
–grower Michael Peterson, Madison, Wisconsin

Originally from East Asia, edamame (ed-ah-MAH-may) is relatively new to North America's home gardeners. It requires a growing season of about 10 weeks.

Edamame is the name given to the immature soybean pod. Once edamame pods mature, harden, and dry, the beans inside are used to make soy milk and tofu. Edamame is a complete protein source and the only vegetable that contains all nine essential amino acids.

PLANTING

Two to 4 weeks before planting, dig 2 inches of aged manure and/or compost into the garden bed. Edamame prefers a pH of 6.0 to 6.5. Test the soil and amend, if necessary.

Sow seeds when the soil is moist and at least 55°F and air temperatures have reached 60°F. Set seeds ¼ to ½ of an inch deep, 2 to 4 inches apart, in rows 2 feet apart. Stagger sowing times; each plant's pods mature at the same time. For a second harvest, plant again about 10 days later. Germination takes 1 to 2 weeks.

CARE

Thin seedlings to 6 inches apart when plants are 4 inches tall.

Weed shallowly to avoid disturbing plants' roots.

Mulch with compost, leaves, or hay to retain moisture and control weeds.

Water regularly with 1 inch per week. Edamame tolerates some drought, but yield may suffer.

Edamame plants reach 2 to 3 feet tall.

> **AVOID PLANTING EDAMAME WHERE LEGUMES (BEANS, PEAS) WERE GROWN IN THE PREVIOUS SEASON.**

WIT & WISDOM

● *Edamame originated in China more than 2,000 years ago.
There it is called* mao dou, *which means "hairy bean."*

● *Today, edamame is considered a Japanese vegetable. In Japanese,*
edamame *means "beans on a branch."*

Stake only if wind conditions require.

DISEASES/PESTS *(see pages 158–166)*
Mexican bean beetles; mildew, powdery; root-knot nematodes; stinkbugs; white mold; whiteflies; wireworms

HARVEST/STORAGE
For best flavor, harvest edamame pods in the evening when they are 2 to 3 inches long, bright green, and plump. Snap or cut (do not tear) pods off plants. Or uproot the entire plant. Yellow pods and/or leaves indicate that the peak of flavor and texture has passed.

Store fresh edamame in an airtight container or plastic bag in the refrigerator for up to 1 week. Use as soon as possible.

To freeze edamame pods or shelled beans, blanch them, plunge them in ice water, and then drain. Store in an airtight bag or container in the freezer.

Harvest dry soybeans when the plant and leaves are dry and brown and the seeds inside the pods rattle. Pull up the plants and hang them in a dark, dry area until the pods are completely dry.

Store dried beans in an airtight container in a dark, cool, dry location.

RECOMMENDED VARIETIES

Edamame is sensitive to day length (light) and classified into "maturity groups" (MG) 00 to 10 (sometimes shown as Roman numerals); the lower the number, the sooner the maturity. Day length is critical to flowering and the production of beans. Low-number varieties are best suited for northern climes; higher-number cultivars, for southern areas. Some suggested varieties:

VARIETIES	MATURITY GROUP	COMMENTS
'Agate'	(MG 00)	buttery flavor
'Black Jet'	(MG 00)	medium-size beans, green when fresh, black when dry; rich flavor
'Envy'	(MG 0)	a short-season favorite
'Early Hakucho'	(MG 1)	compact plant
'Shirofumi 90'	(MG 1)	high yield, over 100 pods per plant
'Madori Giant'	(MG 3)	large beans; high yield
'Gardensoy 51'	(MG 5)	small beans; high yield
'Owens'	(MG 6)	small beans; high yield

EGGPLANT

THE HAPPIEST OMEN
FOR A NEW YEAR IS FIRST MOUNT
FUJI, THEN THE FALCON,
AND LASTLY, EGGPLANT.
–Japanese proverb

Eggplant, aka aubergine, is a perennial "vegetable" grown as an annual that is actually a fruit. The plants make lovely ornamental borders, too.

Eggplant's cousins in the nightshade family include tomatoes and peppers. Like them, it prefers warm temperatures.

PLANTING

Raised beds, which warm more quickly than ground soil, are ideal for growing eggplant. Alternatively, spread a sheet of black plastic on heavy clay soil to warm it before setting out transplants.

Start seeds indoors, ¼ of an inch deep, in flats or peat pots about 6 to 8 weeks before planting time.

One week before planting, mix about 1 inch of aged manure and/or compost or a general fertilizer such as 5-10-5 into the planting bed.

After risk of the last spring frost has passed and daytime temperatures are 70° to 75°F (60° to 65°F at night), set seedlings in holes 24 to 30 inches apart in rows 3 feet apart. Prepare holes by adding 1 tablespoon of 5-10-5 fertilizer or a shovelful of aged manure or rich compost to the bottom of each hole and cover with soil.

If growing in pots, use dark-color containers filled with a premium potting mix, to avoid disease. Put one plant per 5-gallon (or larger) pot in full sun outdoors to facilitate pollination.

Immediately after planting (in ground or pot), set 24-inch-high stakes 1 to 2 inches from each plant or use cages to provide support and avoid disturbing the soil or roots later. Eggplant will fall over when laden with fruit.

Water well. Mulch to retain moisture and suppress weeds.

In cold climates, be prepared to keep plants warm with row covers. Open the ends on warm days to allow bees to pollinate.

CARE

Water consistently; a soaker hose or drip system at ground level is ideal. Strangely shaped eggplants result from inconsistent or inadequate watering.

Apply a balanced fertilizer every 2 weeks or so.

For bigger fruit, pinch out flowers to restrict to five or six per plant.

For a bushier plant, pinch out the terminal growing points, the central points on a plant from which new shoots and leaves grow. Look for the newest (and usually smallest) leaves at the center of the plant and pinch out the bud forming there.

Eggplants are susceptible to temperature fluctuations: Cool nights (below 55°F) or hot days (above 95°F) can cause lack of fruiting. Cover plants on cold nights and provide shade (e.g., a beach umbrella) on hot, sunny days. Cold also impairs ripening.

DISEASES/PESTS *(see pages 158–166)*
Blight, early; blight, late; blossom-end rot; Colorado potato beetles; flea

RECOMMENDED VARIETIES

Eggplant colors range from the familiar dark purple to green, white, pink, and black. Variety sizes and shapes also vary.

'Applegreen': oval, 5- to 6-inch, tender, pale green fruit

'Bambino': oval, walnut-size, purple/black fruit; 1½-foot-tall plants

'Black Bell': classic oval to round, 6-inch, purple/black fruit; disease-resistant

'Casper': cylindrical, 6-inch, snow-white fruit; mushroom flavor

'Cloud Nine': teardrop-shape, 7-inch, white fruit; disease-resistant

'Dusky': classic pear-shape, 6- to 7-inch, glossy purple/black fruit; excellent flavor; disease-resistant

'Ichiban': Japanese type; 10- to 12-inch, slim, purple/black fruit; bears until frost

'Kermit': Thai type; round, 2-inch, green fruit with white-striped shoulder

'Little Fingers': finger-size purple/black fruit; good for containers

'Rosita': pear-shape, 6- to 8-inch, rose-pink fruit; sweet flavor

beetles; mildew, powdery; tomato hornworms; whiteflies

HARVEST/STORAGE

Harvest 16 to 24 weeks after sowing, when the skin of the fruit is shiny and unwrinkled, but do not wait too long to harvest. As soon as the skin does not rebound to gentle pressure from your finger, it's ripe.

When harvesting, cut the fruit with a sharp knife or pruning shears close to the stem, leaving about 1 inch of it attached. Do not pull the fruit; it won't come off.

Eggplants can be stored for up to 2 weeks in humid conditions no lower than 50°F. In the refrigerator, they will keep for several days. Do not wash or cut before refrigerating.

WHEN HARVESTING, DO NOT PULL THE EGGPLANT, BUT CUT IT CLOSE TO THE STEM.

WIT & WISDOM

- *Use a stainless steel knife (not carbon steel) to cut eggplant, or the flesh will discolor.*
- *Eggplant originally came in only small, white varieties. Hanging on the plants, the fruit looked like eggs—hence its name.*

GARLIC

**SHALLOTS ARE FOR BABIES; ONIONS ARE FOR MEN;
GARLIC IS FOR HEROES.**
—Unknown

Garlic is easy to grow. In addition to having an intense flavor and many culinary uses, "the stinking rose" also serves as an insect repellent in the garden, and it has been used as a home remedy for centuries.

Garlic that is planted in the fall is harvested in July and August. A single 10-foot row should yield about 5 pounds of the fragrant bulbs. Set aside a few harvested cloves, because in fall, garlic is planted anew.

PLANTING

For most areas, we advise planting garlic in autumn. Garlic can be planted in spring as soon as the ground can be worked, but the cloves use the fall and winter months to develop roots so that by early spring the roots can support the rapid leaf growth that is necessary to form large bulbs.

One week before planting, mix aged manure and/or compost into the soil. If you have poorly draining, heavy clay soil, transfer the amended soil to a raised bed that is 2 to 3 feet wide and at least 10 to 12 inches deep.

Immediately before planting, work a couple of tablespoons of 5-10-10 complete fertilizer, bonemeal, or fish meal into the soil several inches below where the base

WIT & WISDOM

- *Old-timers say that garlic "learns" because it adapts to your growing conditions and improves each year.*
- *Rub raw garlic on an insect bite to relieve the sting or itching.*

AFTER ONE OR TWO CURLS, GARLIC SCAPES ARE READY FOR CUTTING.

of each garlic clove will rest.

In northern climates, plant between September (after the equinox, usually September 21 or 22) and November. In southern areas, you can plant as late as February or March. The goal is to give the plant time to develop good roots before the ground freezes but not enough time for it to form top growth before freezing temperatures set in. In areas that get a hard frost, plant garlic cloves 6 to 8 weeks before the first fall frost date, before the ground freezes.

Select healthy, large cloves from a seed company, local nursery, or farmers' market. The larger the clove, the bigger the bulb it will produce. (Do not plant cloves from garlic bulbs purchased at a grocery store.) Break apart cloves from the bulb up to 2 days before planting); do not remove their papery husk.

Plant cloves upright (root end down, pointed end up), 4 to 8 inches apart and 2 inches deep, in rows 6 to 12 inches apart. Spacing can vary, based on the garden size and garlic type.

Mulch heavily with straw or leaves to insulate and prevent soil heaving in winter.

CARE

Shoots emerge in spring. After the threat of frost has passed, remove heavy mulch, leaving only enough to deter weeds.

Garlic is a heavy feeder. In early spring, side-dress with or broadcast blood meal, pelleted chicken manure, or a synthetic source of nitrogen.

Fertilize again just before the bulbs begin to swell in response to lengthening daylight (early May in most regions). Repeat if the foliage begins to yellow.

Weed regularly. Garlic needs all available nutrients.

Water every 3 to 5 days during bulbing (mid-May through June). If May and June are dry, irrigate to a depth of 2 feet every 8 to 10 days. As mid-June approaches, taper off watering.

Around the time of the summer

> **GARLIC'S FLAVOR INCREASES AS BULBS DRY.**

solstice, hardneck garlic sends up a seed stalk, or scape. Allow it to curl, then cut off the curl (or leave a couple; see Harvest/Storage) to allow the plant to put its energy into bulb formation. Use the curl, minus the seed head, in the kitchen as you would garlic cloves.

DISEASES/PESTS *(see pages 158–166)*

Onion maggots; thrips, onion; white rot

HARVEST/STORAGE

Harvest garlic when the tops/foliage begin to yellow and fall over, before

RECOMMENDED VARIETIES

There are three types of garlic: hardneck, softneck, and great-headed (aka elephant). Most types are about 90 days to harvest, beginning when growth starts.

Hardneck varieties produce a single ring of fat cloves around a thick, unbendable stem, which forms a curling scape that eventually straightens and develops flowers and bulbils. They have a mild flavor and are extremely cold-hardy but do not store well or long. Varieties include 'Chesnok Red', 'Duganski', 'German Red', 'Korean Red', 'Music', 'Purple Stripe', 'Siberian', and 'Spanish Roja'.

Softneck varieties produce a cluster of cloves but usually no scape; the "neck" remains soft, making them ideal for braiding. Grow softneck in warmer climes; they are less winter-hardy than other types. Bulbs tend to be larger than those of hardnecks, with intense flavor. Varieties include 'Artichoke', 'California Early', 'Inchelium Red', and 'Silverskin'.

Great-headed bulbs are large, with about four cloves each. They are less hardy than other types. Actually being a variety of leek, they have a flavor that is only mildly garlicky.

they are completely dry. Any remaining scapes will have uncurled and be standing up straight. Note that some garlic types are ready before the tops are yellow. To test readiness, lift a bulb. It should have plump cloves covered with a thick, dry, papery skin.

To harvest, dig, don't pull: Lift bulbs with a spade or garden fork and brush off the soil. Be gentle: Bruised garlic does not store well. If lifted too early, the bulb wrapping will be thin and disintegrate. If lifted late, bulbs may split apart and/or skin may tear, exposing cloves. These do not store well.

Cure bulbs in a shady, dry spot with good air circulation for 2 weeks. Lay them in an open box or hang them on a string in bunches of four to six.

Store bulbs when wrappers are dry and papery and roots are dry. The head should be hard, and cloves should crack apart easily. Brush off (do not wash) dirt, remove only the dirtiest wrappers, trim roots to ¼ of an inch, and cut tops to 1 to 2 inches.

Store bulbs in a cool (40°F), dark, dry place (not in a damp basement or the refrigerator). They keep for several months.

Set aside a few large, well-formed bulbs for planting in the next season.

STORE BULBS WHEN WRAPPERS ARE DRY AND PAPERY AND ROOTS ARE DRY.

KALE

[G]ARDENS, OR YARDS, AS THE INHABITANTS CALLED THEM . . .
WERE STORED WITH GIGANTIC PLANTS OF KALE OR COLEWORT . . .
–Waverly, *by Sir Walter Scott, Scottish writer (1771–1832)*

Kale is a hardy, cool-season, nonheading green. It is a cole (mustard family) crop and grows best in spring and fall. It can tolerate fall frosts—even snow.

Kale is a biennial (2-year) plant: It produces leaves in the first year, and then, in the next year (or sometimes late in the first year), it will form a flower stalk. The stalk forms flowers and then seeds. Once the seeds mature, the plant dies.

PLANTING

Plant kale at any time, from early spring to early summer or even in late summer. Late-season harvests can be made until the ground freezes.

Before planting, mix aged manure and/or compost into the soil. If desired, also mix some 5-10-10 fertilizer into the top 3 to 4 inches of soil.

Plant transplants 4 to 6 weeks before the average last spring frost, 12 inches apart, in rows 18 to 24 inches apart.

For a fall crop, direct-seed 3 months before the first fall frost. Plant seeds ¼ to ½ of an inch deep, 1 inch apart, in rows 18 to 30 inches apart.

CARE

After about 2 weeks, thin seedlings to 8 to 12 inches apart.

Water plants regularly with 1 to 1½ inches per week.

Side-dress as needed with a high-nitrogen fertilizer.

WIT & WISDOM

- *Kale is not native to North America. Current varieties are descended from wild cabbage.*
- *Farmers have long grown kale as fodder for farm animals, including cattle and sheep.*

Kale growth can slow if plants are stressed (e.g., are too hot or cold; have inadequate water; have pests or diseases or, if container-grown, crowded roots).

To guarantee a supply of mature leaves through winter, mulch heavily after the first hard freeze.

Once kale bolts, its leaf flavor becomes bitter and harvesting should stop.

DISEASES/PESTS *(see pages 158–166)*
Aphids; black rot; cabbageworms, imported; flea beetles

HARVEST/STORAGE
Harvest kale when leaves are about the size of your hand. Pick about a fistful of outer leaves per harvest, but no more

DO NOT PLANT KALE OR OTHER COLE CROPS IN THE SAME LOCATION MORE THAN ONCE EVERY 3 OR 4 YEARS.

than one-third of the plant at one time. Avoid picking the terminal bud (at the top center of the plant), which helps to maintain the plant's productivity.

Kale will continue growing until temperatures reach 20°F. Do not stop harvesting: A "kiss" of frost makes it even sweeter. To extend the harvest, protect with row covers or tarps.

Store kale like other leafy greens, in a plastic bag in the refrigerator. It should keep for about 1 week.

RECOMMENDED VARIETIES

'Red Russian' (or 'Russian Red'): heirloom; oak leaf–shape, gray-green leaves with deep-purple veins and stem; an early crop

'Lacinato' (aka 'Lacinato Blue', 'Tuscan', 'Black Palm Tree', or 'Cavolo Nero'): heirloom; straplike leaves up to 2 feet long on plants that resemble small palm trees; heat tolerant and very cold-hardy

'True Siberian': large, frilly, blue-green leaves; cold-hardy; pick all winter in some areas

'Vates Blue Curled' (or 'Blue-Curled Vates'): hardy variety that is slow to bolt and does not yellow in cold weather. Its eponymous leaves reach 12 to 14 inches on 15-inch plants.

'Winterbor': resembles 'Vates', with 24-inch leaves on 2- to 3-foot-tall plants; baby leaves can be harvested at 28 days; frost-tolerant

KOHLRABI

IT IS A HYBRID BETWEEN THE CABBAGE AND THE TURNIP, AND WHILE IT HAS FINER FLAVOR THAN EITHER, PARTAKES OF THE QUALITIES OF BOTH.
–John Jay Mapes, American scientist, inventor, and writer (1806–66)

Kohlrabi is a strange-looking vegetable, often overlooked in grocery stores and seed catalogs because of its alien appearance. If given a chance, however, kohlrabi is simple to grow and fast to mature.

A cool-season biennial and part of the Brassica family, kohlrabi is grown for its nutritious, bulb-shape stem.

The globe of crisp, white flesh is sweet and tender—a great addition to salads or stir-fries.

PLANTING
Kohlrabi can be grown as a spring or fall crop.

To start off the growing season, begin sowing kohlrabi seeds in early spring, staggering plantings every 2 to 3 weeks for a continuous summer harvest.

When soil temperatures have reached 45°F, sow seeds ¼ to ½ of an inch deep in rows 10 to 12 inches apart. Once seedlings have emerged (4 to 7 days), thin them to every 5 to 8 inches.

Plant kohlrabi in a location that receives ample sunlight and has rich, slightly acidic, well-draining soil.

Avoid planting kohlrabi where other vegetables in the Brassica family (broccoli, cauliflower, collard greens, kale) have been in the previous 2 or 3 years.

CARE
While kohlrabi is not a heavy feeder, it is helped by having its soil dressed with 1 inch of aged manure and/or compost before planting.

RECOMMENDED VARIETIES

'Early White Vienna', 'Early Purple Vienna': 55–60 days to maturity; sweet and mild

'Gigante': 130 days to maturity; grows up to 10 inches in diameter; stays crisp and sweet

'Grand Duke': 50 days to maturity; can be left in garden without becoming tough

'Kolibri': 45 days to maturity; soft, white flesh; purple-veined leaves

'Korridor': 50 days to maturity; stores longer than most other varieties

'Kossak': 80 days to maturity; grows up to 8 inches in diameter; stores well

'Superschmelz': 60 days to maturity; grows deep roots to withstand drought; best grown in fall

'Winner': 45–60 days to maturity; fresh and fruity flavor

Kohlrabi does best in the cool temperatures of spring and fall—hot summer temperatures will stress the plant and hamper the growth of the bulblike stem.

If humidity is low, help to keep the soil moist by spreading a thin layer of straw or grass clippings around the base of the stem.

Water with 1 inch per week, unless the soil seems to be drying out sooner.

Be diligent about weeding around kohlrabi—it can quickly become overrun.

DISEASES/PESTS (*see pages 158–166*)
Aphids; black rot; cabbage loopers; cabbage root maggots; cabbageworms, imported; clubroot; cutworms; flea beetles; mildew, downy; mildew, powdery; thrips, onion

HARVEST/STORAGE
To harvest, cut the kohlrabi root at ground level when the stems are between 2 and 4 inches in diameter.

The bulblike stem should be succulent, tender, and sweet at this size. If allowed to become too large, it becomes tough and bitter.

Harvested kohlrabi stems can be stored with other root crops in a cool, humid place or in the refrigerator for up to 4 weeks. Remove the leaf stems and wash thoroughly before storing.

WIT & WISDOM

- *"Kohlrabi" comes from the German for "cabbage turnip."*
- *Kohlrabi is a relatively new vegetable, having first been documented about 500 years ago.*
- *In the United States, kohlrabi has been grown since at least as far back as 1806.*

LETTUCE

LETTUCE IS LIKE CONVERSATION;
IT MUST BE FRESH AND CRISP,
SO SPARKLING THAT YOU SCARCELY
NOTICE THE BITTER IN IT.
–My Summer in a Garden, *by Charles
Dudley Warner, American writer (1829–1900)*

Homegrown lettuce is far superior, in both taste and vitamin A content, to the store-bought alternative.

Lettuce is a cool-season crop that grows well in the spring and fall in most regions. Temperatures between 45° and 65°F are ideal. Some lettuce seedlings will even tolerate a light frost. Lettuce prefers 5 to 6 hours of sun but can benefit from afternoon shade when temperatures soar. Because lettuce grows quickly, the best approach is to plant a small amount at a time, staggering the plantings.

PLANTING

In the weeks prior to planting, amend the soil as needed to make it loose and well-draining; when wet, it should be moist but not soggy. Lettuce prefers soil that is high in humus, with plenty of compost. To improve and maintain fertility, mix in organic matter about 1 week before you seed or transplant. Till as needed. Lettuce seeds are tiny; large clods will reduce germination.

For an early crop, start seeds indoors 4 to 6 weeks before the last spring frost. Harden off seedlings for 3 days to a week.

Direct-sowing is recommended as

LETTUCE BENEFITS FROM FREQUENT
LIGHT WATERING.

■ **Loose-leaf types:** Plant or thin to
4 inches apart.

■ **Romaine (cos) and butterhead
(loose-head, Bibb, Boston) types:** Plant
or thin to 8 inches apart.

Set rows of lettuce 12 to 15 inches
apart.

Water, with a mist nozzle, if possible,
when seeding or transplanting.

Mulch (if slugs are not a problem) to
suppress weeds, conserve moisture, and
keep the soil cool.

Sow additional seeds every 2 weeks for
a continuous harvest.

For a fall crop, cool the soil in August
by moistening it and covering it with
a bale of straw. One week later, the soil
under the bale should be a few degrees
cooler than the rest of the garden and
ready to be sown with a 2-foot row of
lettuce. Repeat the process every couple
of weeks by rotating the straw bale
around the garden.

As autumn temperatures decline, seed
as usual for a fall harvest.

soon as the ground can be worked. Plant
seeds ⅛ to ½ of an inch deep (seeds
need light to germinate, so not too deep;
follow the guidance on seed packets).

Seed may be sown in single rows or
broadcast for wide row planting (loose-
leaf varieties are best for this). When
broadcasting, thin 1- to 2-inch-tall
seedlings for the proper spacing.

Transplant seedlings into the garden
between 2 weeks before and 2 weeks
after the last spring frost.

■ **Crisphead (iceberg) types:** Plant or
thin to 16 inches apart.

CARE

Fertilize with organic alfalfa meal or
another slow-release fertilizer 3 weeks
after transplanting, to provide a steady
supply of nitrogen.

Observe lettuce to assess its water
needs: If leaves are wilting, sprinkle
them at any time, even in the heat of
the day, to cool them off and slow down
the transpiration rate. Cover plants with
row covers to reduce soil evaporation
and keep plants from frying, wet or dry,
in the heat of the day.

Frequent light watering can result in

RECOMMENDED VARIETIES

Crisphead (iceberg): 'Great Lakes', 'Ithaca', 'Mission', 'Summertime'

Loose-leaf: 'Black Seeded Simpson', 'Green Ice', 'Ibis', 'Lollo Rossa', 'New Red Fire', 'Oak Leaf', 'Prizehead', 'Red Sails', 'Ruby Red', 'Salad Bowl', 'Slobolt'

Romaine (cos)/ butterhead: 'Burpee Bibb', 'Cosmo Savoy', 'Green Towers', 'Little Gem', 'Paris White Cos', 'Parris Island', 'Valmaine'

rapidly developing, high-quality lettuce. Overwatering, especially in nondraining, heavy soils, can lead to disease or soft growth.

Weed by hand; lettuce plants have shallow roots.

Lettuce is bolting if it forms a central/seed stalk, with leaves along the stem and flowers near the top that eventually bear seeds. Bolting can be triggered by heat (over 70°F) or changing day length. During this time, lettuce leaves develop a bitter flavor. To delay bolting, cover plants with shade cloth so that they get filtered light and maintain watering. Planting lettuce in the shade of taller plants—for example, tomatoes or sweet corn—may reduce bolting.

DISEASES/PESTS *(see pages 158–166)*
Aphids; cutworms; earwigs, European; mildew, powdery; mosaic virus, lettuce; slugs/snails; white mold; whiteflies

HARVEST/STORAGE
Harvest lettuce in the morning, when full-size but young and tender.

■ **Crisphead (iceberg) types:** Harvest when the center is firm.

■ **Loose-leaf types:** Remove outer leaves so that the center leaves can continue to grow.

■ **Romaine (cos) and butterhead types:** Remove outer leaves; dig up the whole plant or cut the plant about 1 inch above the soil surface (this might result in a second harvest).

Store lettuce in a loose plastic bag in the refrigerator for up to 10 days.

PLANT ROWS OF CHIVES OR GARLIC BETWEEN LETTUCE PLANTS/ ROWS TO CONTROL OR PREVENT APHIDS.

WIT & WISDOM
- *Lettuce is a member of the daisy family.*
- *To rejuvenate wilted lettuce leaves, put them into a bowl of cold water with ice cubes for about 15 minutes.*
- *Eating lettuce for dinner can be calming and help to reduce stress.*

YOU CAN HAVE STRIP POKRA—GIVE ME A NICE GIRL AND A DISH OF OKRA.
—Roy Blount Jr., American novelist and humorist (b. 1941)

Okra thrives in warm weather and is traditionally grown in the U.S. South. Easy to grow and use, it has beautiful flowers that look great throughout the growing season. It's also rich in vitamin A and low in calories.

PLANTING

Before planting, mix aged manure and/or compost into the soil and amend as needed to make it well-draining.

Okra's BB pellet–size seeds have a hard shell. To speed germination, before sowing, soak seeds for a few hours in fresh water.

Where summers are short, start okra seeds indoors in peat pots under full light 3 to 4 weeks before the last spring frost. Or sow okra directly in the garden 3 to 4 weeks before the last spring frost and then cover the plants with a 2- to 3-foot-high cold frame or grow tunnel until warm weather arrives.

To direct-sow without protection from the cold, wait until the soil is 65° to 70°F. Plant okra in full sun. Set seeds ½ to 1 inch deep and 12 to 18 inches apart. Set okra transplants 1 to 2 feet apart. Space rows 3 to 4 feet apart.

CARE

Eliminate weeds when plants are young, then mulch heavily—4 to 8 inches—to prevent more weeds.

Side-dress plants with 10-10-10 fertilizer, aged manure, or compost. If desired, apply a balanced liquid fertilizer monthly. Avoid too much nitrogen, which can deter flowering and encourage leafy growth.

When seedlings are about 3 inches tall, thin plants to 18 to 24 inches apart.

Water well with 1 inch per week and more in hot, arid regions.

High heat can cause okra growth to slow. Prune the tops of okra plants when

RECOMMENDED VARIETIES

Dwarf types, which seldom exceed 5 feet in height, are best for containers. Standard varieties can top 8 feet or more.

'Blondy': spineless; dwarf at 3 feet tall; pale green 3-inch pods; ideal for northern growers

'Burgundy': abundant 6- to 8-inch pods (harvest at 3 inches) on 3- to 5-foot-tall plants; edible ornamental, with deep red stem, branches, leaf ribs, and fruit

'Cajun Jewel': dwarf at 2½ to 4 feet tall; tasty 8-inch pods up to 1 inch in diameter

'Clemson Spineless': tasty 6½- to 9-inch pods on 4-foot-tall plants

'Louisiana Green Velvet': spineless; vigorous to 6 feet tall

they reach 5 to 6 feet tall. This will result in more side branches; prune those as needed. In warm regions, some growers cut plants to about 2 feet when productivity slows in summer. The plants grow back and produce another crop of okra.

Okra has large, hairy leaves, as well as

WIT & WISDOM

- *Okra is sometimes called "lady's fingers" due to its pods' long, slender shape.*
- *Thomas Jefferson determined freshness by bending the pod: If it gave, it was too old. If it broke, it was just right.*

TO HARVEST OKRA, CUT THE STEM JUST ABOVE THE CAP.

tiny spines on its pods, both of which may cause skin irritation; consider wearing gloves and/or long sleeves when handling. "Spineless" types have pods that don't present this problem. Regardless of type, irritation doesn't occur when you eat okra.

DISEASES/PESTS *(see pages 158–166)*
Aphids; Fusarium wilt; Japanese beetles; mildew, powdery; root-knot nematodes; stinkbugs; whiteflies

IF AN OKRA STEM IS TOO HARD TO CUT, THE POD IS PROBABLY OLD. DRY IT OUT AND USE IT IN FLORAL ARRANGEMENTS OR SAVE THE SEEDS FOR NEXT YEAR.

HARVEST/STORAGE
Seedpods that are 1 to 2 days old and 2 to 4 inches long are softest and most digestible; these appear about 2 months after planting. Cut the stem with a knife just above the cap.

Harvest often: The more you pick, the more flowers will appear, and okra goes from flower to fruit in a few days.

A severe freeze can damage pods. If one is expected and pods are drying on the plant for seeds, cut the plant and hang it indoors to dry. Put a paper bag over it so that if pods shatter, seeds will not be lost.

To store okra, put uncut, raw pods into freezer bags and freeze. Or wash and blanch okra before freezing. Or can it.

ONIONS

An onion can make people cry, but there's never been a vegetable that can make people laugh.
—Will Rogers, American humorist (1879–1935)

Onions are a cold season crop that is easy to grow. Typically, they are planted early in the spring and harvested in the fall after their tops begin to die back. In the southern United States, some onion varieties can be planted in autumn.

Onion sets are tiny onions that mature in about 14 weeks. They can withstand light freezes and have a higher success rate than direct-sown or transplants.

Onions grown from seed require the soil to be at least 50°F to germinate, so these should be started indoors about 6 weeks before transplanting to the garden.

PLANTING

Select a location with full sun. In early spring, before planting, mix aged manure or compost into the soil. Soil needs to be well-draining and loose; compact soil affects bulb development. Raised beds or rows should be at least 4 inches deep.

Onion plants are heavy feeders and require constant nourishment to produce big bulbs. At planting time, add

WIT & WISDOM

- *In the Middle Ages, it was believed that onion juice could cure baldness, snakebite, and headaches.*
- *A generation or two ago, children were treated with a poultice of mashed onions applied as a paste to cover a wound.*
- *A whole onion eaten at bedtime was prescribed to break a cold by morning, and sliced onions were placed on the soles of the feet to draw out fever.*
- *Early settlers made a cough syrup by steeping raw onion slices in honey overnight.*
- *A raw onion rubbed on a bee sting or insect bite will relieve the pain and itching.*

ONIONS CAN LOOK HEALTHY EVEN WHEN THEY ARE BONE-DRY, SO DO WATER DURING DROUGHT CONDITIONS.

nitrogen fertilizer to the soil.

Choose onion sets that are ¾ of an inch in diameter; larger ones tend to produce stiff necks and go to seed. Plant as soon as the ground can be worked in spring, usually late March or April, when temperatures are no longer likely to dip below 28°F. Bury sets 2 to 6 inches apart, gently pressing them into loose soil no more than 1 inch deep. (Use the closer spacing if you want to pull immature onions as scallions.) Space transplants 4 to 5 inches apart and rows 12 to 18 inches apart.

Mulch with straw between rows to help to retain moisture and stifle weeds.

CARE

Think of onions as a leaf crop, not a root crop.

Cover immature bulbs with light mulch to protect them, retain moisture, suppress weeds, and allow air circulation.

Do not cover emerging onions.

Fertilize every few weeks with nitrogen to get big bulbs. Stop fertilizing when the onions push the soil away and bulbing has started.

Generally, if mulch is used, onions do not need consistent watering. Water with about 1 inch per week. For sweeter onions, water more. To deter bolting, water often during hot spells.

To protect against onion maggots, use row covers, sealed at the edges, and rotate crops.

To deter thrips, intercrop onions with tomatoes or carrots in closely alternating rows.

DISEASES/PESTS *(see pages 158–166)*
Onion maggots; thrips, onion; white rot

HARVEST/STORAGE
Pull onions that send up flower stalks; they have stopped growing. These onions will not store well; use them within a few days.

When onions start to mature, the tops (foliage) become yellow and begin to fall over. Bend the tops down (even stomp on them!) to speed the ripening process.

Loosen soil around the bulbs to encourage drying.

Harvest by late summer in dry weather. (Wet-harvested onions do not cure well and might rot in storage.) Mature onions may spoil in cool fall weather.

When tops are brown, pull the onions. Handle them carefully; the slightest bruise (now and in storage) will encourage rot. Cut the roots. Trim the tops back to 1 to 2 inches (unless you plan to braid them).

Set onions on dry ground for a few days to cure, weather permitting, or in a protected place (garage, barn, etc.).

Once cured, hang in a mesh bag; spread up to two layers deep in a box; or braid and hang in a cool (40° to 60°F), dry, well-ventilated area. (Do not store onions in a refrigerator; conditions are too damp.) Check periodically for sprouting or rotting onions and remove them.

Do not store onions with apples or pears; ethylene gas produced by the fruit will interrupt the onions' dormancy. Onions may also spoil the flavor of these fruit and that of potatoes.

Sweet onions have high water content; they do not keep well.

RECOMMENDED VARIETIES

Onions are photoperiodic, or sensitive to daylight, so different varieties have been bred for varying day lengths. The border between long- and short-day varieties lies roughly at 36 degrees north latitude. North of that, plant long-day types; south of it, plant short-day onions. Or try "day-neutral" (intermediate) varieties, which yield an excellent crop anywhere, regardless of day length.

Long-day varieties . . .

'Ailsa Craig', 'Walla Walla': huge bulbs

'Buffalo', 'Norstar': produce early but keep only until late December

'Copra', 'Southport Red Globe', 'Sweet Sandwich', 'Yellow Globe': keep well

'Red Florence': oblong shape

Short-day varieties . . .

'Crystal Wax White Bermuda': a pickler when picked at pearl size

'Hybrid Yellow Granex': sweet, Vidalia type

'Red Burgundy': mild, sweet, white inside, short-term keeper

'Southern Belle': ruby-color throughout

'Texas 1015-Y Supersweet': stores well

Day-neutral, or intermediate, varieties . . .

'Candy': golden, thick-flesh, jumbo bulbs; stores well

'Red Stockton': large, red-ringed, white flesh bulbs

'Super Star': large, sweet, white bulbs

PARSNIPS

THE PARSNIP, CHILDREN, I REPEAT,
IS MERELY AN ANEMIC BEET.
–Ogden Nash, American poet (1902–71)

Parsnips are a hardy, cool-season biennial crop that is usually grown as an annual vegetable. It is planted in spring, kissed by frost, and harvested before the ground freezes.

Parsnips enrich soups and stews but can also be enjoyed as a side dish.

PLANTING

Parsnips need a long growing season; if planted too late in the season, its roots will be small. Direct-seed as soon as the soil is workable and at least 48°F, but ideally 50° to 54°F (this will speed germination). Do not plant where sod grew in the previous season. Excess nitrogen in the soil will cause overabundant top growth and poor roots. Do a soil test.

Prior to planting, loosen the soil to a depth of 12 to 15 inches and mix in aged manure and/or compost.

Sow seeds ½ of an inch deep, 1 inch apart, in rows 18 to 24 inches wide.

Germination is slow: Seedlings emerge in 2 to 3 weeks. To hasten the process, keep the soil moist. To expedite germination, start by soaking paper towels or cotton wool pads. Place them on a saucer and press papery parsnip seeds into them. Keep the seeds warm (50° to 54°F) and

ALWAYS SOW FRESH SEED; PARSNIP SEEDS DO NOT STORE WELL.

watch for little white roots to appear. Then sow as described; discard any seeds that fail.

If desired, sow radish seeds alongside to mark rows and break the dirt's crust.

Thin seedlings to 3 to 4 inches: To avoid disturbing neighbor plants, cut off tops; do not pull seedlings.

Mulch to retain moisture and suppress weeds.

CARE

Water in summer if rainfall is less than 1 inch per week.

Weed regularly.

Use row covers to deter pests.

Hill soil around the plants' base to prevent greening of the roots' shoulders.

Be careful about handling parsnips, as the sap and/or leaves can be irritating to the skin. Wear long pants, long sleeves, and gloves when weeding or harvesting.

DISEASES/PESTS *(see pages 158–166)*
Aphids, black (Itersonilia) canker, carrot rust flies, leaf miners

HARVEST/STORAGE
Parsnips mature in about 16 weeks.

When exposed to near-freezing temperatures for 2 to 4 weeks in the fall/early winter, the starch in the root changes into sugar, resulting in a strong, sweet, unique taste. Leave parsnips in

RECOMMENDED VARIETIES

Choose short-root varieties for soil that is shallow, heavy, and/or has stones.

'All-American': tapered, 10- to 12-inch white roots; high sugar content; stores well

'Harris Model': smooth, tapered, average 10-inch white roots, free of side roots

'Hollow Crown': mild, 12-inch white, fine-grain roots; flavor develops after frost

'Kral Russian': heirloom; beet-shape root; good for shallow or heavy soil

the ground for a few frosts but harvest before the ground freezes. Or leave them in the ground for the entire winter, covered with a thick layer of mulch. Harvest immediately after the ground thaws in spring, before top growth starts. If a flower stalk develops, root quality may suffer, turning woody.

Before storing roots, trim off leaves, down to 2 to 3 inches.

Store parsnips at 32° to 35°F, with 90 to 95 percent humidity. For long-term storage (4 to 6 months), store roots in slightly damp sand, sawdust, or leaves.

WIT & WISDOM

• *Soft words butter no parsnips, but they won't harden the heart of the cabbage either.*
–Irish proverb

• *Popular with ancient Greeks and Romans, parsnips came to the Americas with the first colonists.*

PEAS

**PEAS WENT WITH CARROTS AS INFALLIBLY AS HAM WENT WITH EGGS.
FOR YEARS, I THOUGHT THAT CARROTS AND PEAS GREW ON THE SAME VINE.**
–Ruth Eleanor "Peg" Bracken, American humorist (1918–2007)

Peas are one of the season's first crops. Plant them as soon as the ground can be worked—even if snow falls afterward. Peas are easy to grow, but their growing period is very limited. Plus, peas do not stay fresh long after harvest, so enjoy them while you can!

Three varieties of peas suit most garden and culinary needs:

■ Sweet peas, aka English peas or garden peas (*Pisum sativum* ssp. *sativum*), have inedible pods from which the seeds (peas) are taken.

■ Snow peas (*P. sativum* var. *macrocarpon*) have edible, flat, stringless pods containing small peas.

■ Snap peas (*P. sativum* var. *macrocarpon* ser. cv.) have thick, edible pods containing large/full-size peas.

PLANTING

In the fall prior to planting, turn over the pea bed, mix in aged manure and/

WIT & WISDOM

● *St. Patrick's Day (March 17) is a traditional day for planting peas.*

● *Legend has it that the phrase "green thumb" originated during the reign of King Edward I of England, who was fond of green peas and kept six serfs shelling them in season. The serf who had the greenest thumb won a prize.*

---

or compost, and mulch well. Peas like well-draining soil. (Rotate crops: Do not plant peas in the same place more than once in every 4 years.) Pea roots, like those of other legumes, fix nitrogen in the soil, making it available for other plants. Adding nitrogen fertilizer promotes lush foliage but risks poor flowering and fruiting.

If available, mix wood ashes or bonemeal into the soil before planting.

Sow seeds 4 to 6 weeks before the last spring frost, while the soil is cool, or when it is at the desired temperature: Peas planted in cold (40°F) soil will germinate slowly; peas planted in soil that is at least 60°F (but not more than 85°F) will catch up. To speed germination, soak seeds in a bowl of water overnight.

Sow seeds 1 inch deep (deeper, if the soil is dry) and 2 inches apart. Do not thin.

Although peas do not like their roots disturbed, transplanting is possible. Start seeds in peat pots. Transplant, pot and all, into the garden; the pot will disintegrate.

Where the spring is long and wet, plant in raised beds.

Snow will not hurt emerging pea plants, but several days with temperatures in the teens might. Be prepared to plant again.

Bush peas can reach 18 to 30 inches tall. Pole types can grow to at least 4 to 6 feet tall. Both benefit from support (especially bush peas above 2 feet and all pole peas). Install thin tree branches (pea sticks), trellises, chicken wire, or netting before plants establish their shallow roots.

Water to keep the soil moist. If seeds wash out of the soil, poke them back into it.

RECOMMENDED VARIETIES

'Green Arrow': sweet/shelling; 2- to 3-foot vines; no support required; high yields, tolerance of mildew and Fusarium wilt

'Lincoln': sweet/shelling; 2½- to 3-foot vines; no support required; tolerance of mildew and Fusarium wilt

'Mammoth Melting': snow pea; 4- to 5-foot vines; stringless pods

'Sugar Ann': snap pea; 2-foot vines; no support required

CARE

Water sparsely with no more than 1 inch per week, unless plants are wilting. Do not let plants dry out; if this happens, no pods will be produced.

If necessary, hoe or cultivate carefully to avoid disturbing peas' shallow, fragile roots.

Pea leaves turn yellow for several reasons. Often, this is due to the stress of hot weather. Provide partial shade (e.g., row covers) during the hottest time of day and water properly.

DISEASES/PESTS *(see pages 158–166)*
Aphids; Fusarium wilt; mildew, downy; mildew, powdery; root-knot nematodes; wireworms

HARVEST/STORAGE
Harvest peas in the morning after the dew has dried and regularly to encourage more pods to develop. Use

> IF YOUR PEAS' PEAK FLAVOR PERIOD PASSES, PICK, DRY, AND SHELL PEAS FOR USE IN WINTER SOUPS.

two hands when harvesting: Hold the vine with one hand and pull pods off with the other. Peas are at the peak of flavor immediately after harvest.

Store peas in the refrigerator for about 5 days: Place in paper bags, then wrap in plastic. Or freeze: Shell sweet peas, blanch, immerse in cold water, drain, and pack in sealed containers. De-string/trim snow or snap peas and prepare as above.

PICK REGULARLY TO ENCOURAGE THE DEVELOPMENT OF MORE PODS.

BELL PEPPERS

I LOVE RED BELL PEPPERS. BELL PEPPERS IN GENERAL, REALLY. I LIKE TO EAT
THEM LIKE APPLES. THEY'RE SO CRUNCHY AND DELICIOUS.

–Alex Honnold, American professional rock climber (b. 1985)

Peppers are a tender, warm-season crop that comes in a variety of colors, shapes, and sizes. More good news: Most varieties resist garden pests.

PLANTING

Start pepper seeds (¼ of an inch deep, three to a pot) indoors 8 to 10 weeks before the last spring frost date. For fast germination, maintain seeds at 70°F or above. Thin out the weakest seedling; let the remaining two pepper plants in each pot grow as one. The leaves of two plants help to protect peppers against sunscald, and the yield is often greater than that from two separate plants.

Northern gardeners should warm soil by covering it with black plastic as early as possible in late winter/early spring.

Begin to harden off seedlings about 10 days before transplanting.

A week before transplanting, mix aged manure and/or compost into the garden. Peppers like well-draining moist (not wet) soil.

After the danger of frost has passed and the soil has reached 65°F (peppers will not survive colder soil), transplant seedlings, 18 to 24 inches apart, keeping paired plants close to touching. Avoid disturbing the roots. Into each hole put two or three wooden matchsticks (for sulfur) and 1 teaspoon of low-nitrogen, high-phosphorus fertilizer (too much nitrogen will reduce fruit set).

Stake now to avoid disturbing the roots later.

CARE

Water regularly with 1 to 2 inches per

week. Provide more or less water only when temperature and/or humidity changes drastically. In a warm or desert climate, water every day, if necessary. Note that in desert regions at around 4,000 feet of elevation, sweet bell peppers often fail to develop a thick, fleshy wall.

Peppers are extremely heat sensitive. Blossoms may drop if plants are stressed—if it's too hot (above 85° to 90°F in daytime) or cold (below 60°F at night) or water is inadequate. Poor pollination, nutrient-rich or -poor soil, and pests can also cause bloom loss.

Sunscalded peppers can appear faded, papery, blistered, or gray-white and sunken. Use shade cloth or row covers to avoid sunscald when fruit is exposed to sunlight during hot, humid weather.

RECOMMENDED VARIETIES

Look for varieties that ripen to full color quickly. Fully mature peppers are the most nutritious and tastiest.

Green peppers that turn red: 'Bell Boy', 'Gypsy', 'Lady Bell', 'Lipstick'

Orange peppers: 'Milena', 'Orange Sun'

Yellow pepper: 'Golden California Wonder'

Fruit should develop under the leaves.

Mulch to maintain moisture and deter weeds.

After the first fruit set, sprinkle 1 tablespoon of Epsom salts around each plant (the salts contain beneficial sulfur and magnesium). Or spray with a solution of 1 tablespoon of Epsom salts in 1 gallon of water.

Weed carefully to avoid disturbing roots.

When fruit is full-size but not yet ripe, reduce water to speed maturing.

DISEASES/PESTS *(see pages 158–166)*
Anthracnose; aphids; blossom-end rot; Colorado potato beetles; flea beetles; mosaic virus, cucumber; root-knot nematodes; tomato hornworms

HARVEST/STORAGE
Harvest when peppers reach desired size and color. Use a sharp knife or scissors to cut peppers off the plant.

Refrigerate fruit in plastic bags for up to 10 days.

Bell peppers can be dried: Preheat the oven to 140°F (or lowest temperature). Wash, core, and seed peppers. Cut into ½-inch strips. Steam for about 10 minutes, then spread on a baking sheet. Dry in oven until desired condition (about 4 to 6 hours); turn occasionally and switch tray positions. Cool, then store in bags or containers in a refrigerator.

WIT & WISDOM

- *Unlike hot peppers, bell peppers do not contain capsaicin, the compound that generates pungency and heat.*
- *The longer a bell pepper stays on the plant, the greater its vitamin C content.*

POTATOES

**WHAT I SAY IS THAT IF A MAN REALLY LIKES POTATOES,
HE MUST BE A PRETTY DECENT SORT OF FELLOW.**
–A. A. Milne, English writer (1882–1956)

The taste and the texture of home-grown potatoes are far superior to those of store-bought spuds, especially the early varieties—and garden "taters" provide a bounty of nutrients!

Potatoes like sunny, cool weather and well-drained, loose soil at 45° to 55°F. In warmer climates, potatoes can be grown as a winter crop.

PLANTING

Potatoes can be planted 2 weeks after the last spring frost or as soon as the soil can be worked, but be aware that early crops may be ruined by a frost or wet soil. If you have a late spring, you can plant later—through April (depending on location) or even June, especially in containers.

Use certified (disease-resistant) seed potatoes from which eyes (buds) protrude. (Do not confuse seed potatoes with potato seeds or grocery produce.)

One to 2 days before planting, cut large potatoes into golf ball–size pieces, with 1 to 2 eyes each. The time allows the pieces to heal, or form a protective layer over the cut surface, improving both moisture retention and rot resistance. Do not cut up seed potatoes that are smaller than a hen's egg; plant them whole.

Potatoes grow best in rows about 3 feet apart. With a hoe or round-point

WIT & WISDOM

• In New England, growers plant potato crops when dandelions bloom.
• Grated raw potato is said to soothe sunburned skin.
• Want to root a rose? Push the cut stem into a raw potato and plant them both in the garden.

HILLING KEEPS POTATOES FROM GETTING SUNBURNED, WHICH CAN CAUSE THEM TO TURN GREEN AND PRODUCE A BITTER, TOXIC CHEMICAL.

shovel, dig a trench row about 6 inches wide and 8 inches deep. Taper the bottom to about 3 inches wide. Spread and mix in aged manure, compost, and/or leaves. Place a seed potato piece, cut side down, every 12 to 14 inches. Cover with 3 to 4 inches of soil.

In 12 to 16 days, when sprouts appear, gently fill in the trench with 3 to 4 inches of soil, leaving a few inches of the plants exposed. Repeat as they grow until the trench is at ground level.

Mulch between rows to conserve moisture, control weeds, and cool the soil.

Got really rocky ground? Put sprouted seed potato pieces on the soil surface. Mix together soil and compost, sprinkle it on top, and then cover with straw and/or

leaves—8 inches in total. Follow the Care tips. Hill with soil and compost as the potatoes grow. Hilling keeps sunlight off the spuds; they will turn green if exposed. To harvest, push aside the organic matter.

CARE

Maintain even moisture, especially from the time that sprouts appear until several weeks after the flowers bloom. Potatoes need 1 to 2 inches of water per week. Too much water right after planting and not enough as the potatoes begin to form can cause them to become misshapen. Stop watering when the foliage begins to turn yellow and die off.

Hill in the mornings, until the soil is mounded 4 to 5 inches above the ground. Hoe dirt up around the base of the plant to cover the tubers and support the plant. Stop hilling when the plant is about 6 inches tall, before blooms appear. Hilling keeps potatoes from getting sunburned, which can cause them to turn green and produce a chemical called solanine. Solanine gives off a bitter taste and is toxic.

"Berries" appear on potato vines during cool growing seasons. They are fruit; cut one open and see how it resembles its cousin, the tomato. The berries are not edible and will not produce potato plants that resemble the parent. They are poisonous; discard them.

DO NOT PLANT POTATOES WHERE THEY THEMSELVES OR THEIR COUSINS EGGPLANTS, PEPPERS, OR TOMATOES HAVE BEEN GROWN IN THE PAST 2 YEARS.

DISEASES/PESTS *(see pages 158–166)*
Aphids; blight, early; blight, late; Colorado potato beetles; flea beetles; leafhoppers; potato scab, common; tomato hornworms; viruses; whiteflies; wireworms

HARVEST/STORAGE
Harvest potatoes on dry days. Dig up gently, being careful not to puncture the tubers. Avoid cutting or bruising potato skin. The soil should not be compact, so digging should be easy. If the soil is very wet, let potatoes air-dry before putting them into bags or baskets.

Harvest "new" potatoes, small ones with tender skin, 2 to 3 weeks after plants stop flowering. Eat new potatoes within a few days (curing is not necessary); they will not keep for much longer.

Harvest larger, more mature potatoes 2 to 3 weeks after the foliage has died. Cut down the brown foliage.

Put freshly dug potatoes in a dry, cool place (45° to 60°F) for up to 2 weeks to allow the skin to cure and thus keep longer. Brush off any clinging soil, then store in a cool (38° to 40°F), somewhat humid, dark place.

Do not store potatoes with apples; the fruits' ethylene gas causes potatoes to spoil. Never store potatoes in the refrigerator.

Avoid washing potatoes, which will shorten their storage life.

RECOMMENDED VARIETIES

Potato varieties number more than 100. Tan-skin and red-skin varieties with white flesh are the most common in home gardens. Plant varieties with different harvest times to enjoy them all season long.

Early varieties . . .

'Irish Cobbler': tan skin; irregular shape

'Norland': red skin; resistant to potato scab

'Mountain Rose': red skin and pink flesh; resistant to some viruses

Midseason varieties . . .

'Red Pontiac': red skin; deep eyes

'Viking': red skin; very productive

'Chieftain': red skin; resistant to potato scab; stores well

Late varieties . . .

'Katahdin': tan skin; resistant to some viruses

'Kennebec': tan skin; resistant to some viruses and late blight

'Elba': tan skin; large, round tubers; resistant to blight and potato scab

PUMPKINS

**ONE CAN NOT MANAGE TOO MANY AFFAIRS; LIKE PUMPKINS IN WATER,
ONE POPS UP WHILE YOU TRY TO HOLD DOWN THE OTHER.**
—Chinese proverb

Whether you use them for carving or cooking, pumpkins do not disappoint—if you have the space to grow them.

Pumpkins require a lot of nourishment and a long growing season (generally from 75 to 100 frost-free days). Growers in northern locations need to plant them by late May; in extremely southern states, early July. That said, pumpkins are easy to maintain.

PLANTING
Pick a spot in full sun (to light shade) with space for sprawling vines to run:

50 to 100 square feet per hill. If space is limited, plant at the edge of the garden and direct vine growth across the lawn. Vines will be bothersome for only a few weeks. In very limited space, grow pumpkins in 10-, 12-, or 15-gallon buckets (depending on variety) or try miniature varieties.

Mix aged manure and/or compost into the soil to plant in rows 6 to 10 feet apart. Or plant in hills 4 to 8 feet apart. Hills warm soil quickly (so seeds germinate faster) and aid with drainage and pest control. Prepare hills by digging down 12 to 15 inches and mixing/filling in with lots of aged manure and/or compost.

Sow seeds directly after danger of frost has passed and the soil is between 65° and 95°F, the optimum temperature range. (If the soil is at 70°F, seedlings should emerge in 5 to 10 days.)

In rows, sow seeds 6 to 12 inches apart. Thin to one plant every 18 to 36 inches.

In hills, set seeds 1 inch deep with four or five seeds per hill. Keep seeds moist until germination. When seedlings are 2 to 3 inches tall, thin to two or three per hill by snipping out unwanted plants.

Where the growing season is very short, sow indoors in peat pots, 2 to 4 weeks before last spring frost. Harden off seedlings before transplanting into warm, aged manure/compost–enriched soil.

CARE

Use row covers to protect plants early in the season and to prevent insect problems. Remove covers before flowering to allow pollination. To attract bees, place a bee house in the garden or grow colorful flowers near the patch.

Pumpkins need 1 inch of water per week. Water deeply, in the morning and on very hot afternoons, especially during fruit set. Avoid watering foliage and fruit unless it's a sunny day. Dampness invites rot and diseases.

RECOMMENDED VARIETIES

Miniature pumpkins: 'Jack Be Little', 'Munchkin', 'We-B-Little'

Pumpkin for carving/decorating: 'Autumn Gold'

For giant pumpkins: 'Dill's Atlantic Giant'

Pumpkins for pies: 'Baby Bear', 'Cinderella's Carriage', 'Hijinks', 'Peanut Pumpkin', 'Sugar Treat'

Colorful pumpkins: 'Jarrahdale' (blue-green skin), 'Pepitas Pumpkin' (orange and green), 'Super Moon' (large white pumpkin)

Mulch around plants to retain moisture, discourage pests, and suppress weeds. Weed gently; pumpkins have shallow roots that can be easily damaged. Also, take care not to damage the delicate vines; the quality of fruit depends on them.

Small vine varieties can be trained to grow up a trellis. Larger varieties can be trained upward, too; to support the fruit, try using netting or old stockings.

First flowers often do not form fruit. Both male and female blossoms need to open. Be patient.

Be aware that poor light, too much fertilizer, poor weather at bloom time, and reduced pollinating insect activity

> **HOPING FOR A PRIZE PUMPKIN? SELECT TWO OR THREE PRIME CANDIDATES, THEN REMOVE ALL OTHER FRUIT AND PINCH VINES.**

can result in poor fruit set and shape and excessive blossom drop.

Pumpkins are heavy feeders. Side-dress with aged manure or compost mixed with water. When plants are about 1 foot tall, just before vines begin to run, fertilize regularly with a high-nitrogen formula. Just before the blooming period, switch to a high-phosphorous fertilizer.

After a few pumpkins have formed, pinch off the fuzzy ends of each vine to stop vine growth and focus plant energy on the fruit.

Pruning vines may help with space and fruit formation. Pumpkins produce main vines (from the base/

center of the plant), secondary vines off the main ones, and tertiary vines off the secondaries. All may have flowers. Once fruit has started to develop, prune the main and secondary vines to 10 to 15 feet (bury the cut tips in soil) and remove the tertiary vines, if desired. Or trim the main and secondaries to two or three pumpkins and retain several feet of vine/leaves beyond the last fruit.

As fruit develop, turn them—with great care not to hurt the vine or stem—to encourage an even shape. Slip a thin board or a piece of plastic mesh under pumpkins to protect them.

To grow a giant pumpkin, try the 'Dill's Atlantic Giant' jumbo variety. Fruit can grow to 200 pounds on 25-foot vines. Plants need 130 to 160 days to mature, so start seedlings indoors, then thin to the best one or two plants. Feed heavily and cultivate shallowly. Remove the first two or three female flowers to generate more leaf surface before a plant sets fruit. Allow one fruit to develop; remove all other female flowers. Take care that the vine does not root down near the joints to avoid breakage.

DISEASES/PESTS (*see pages 158–166*)
Anthracnose; aphids; cucumber beetles; mildew, downy; mildew, powdery; squash bugs; squash vine borer

---

WIT & WISDOM

- *A slice of pumpkin pie before bedtime may help you to sleep.*
- *Pumpkin halves were supposedly used as guides for haircuts in colonial New Haven, Connecticut, giving rise to the nickname "pumpkinhead."*

HARVEST/STORAGE

Harvest pumpkins when they reach maturity—and not before. (If you want small pumpkins, grow a small variety.) The skin of a ripening pumpkin turns a deep, solid color (orange for most varieties) and the stem hardens. Thump the pumpkin; the rind will feel hard and sound hollow. Press a fingernail into the skin; if it resists puncture, it is ripe.

Carefully cut the fruit off the vine with a sharp knife or pruners; do not tear it. Leave 3 to 4 inches of stem to increase its keeping time.

Pumpkins bruise easily; handle them gently.

To toughen the skin and intensify flavor, cure pumpkins in a sunny spot for a week or so or in an area that is 80° to 85°F, with 80 to 85 percent humidity, for 10 days. After curing, store in a cool, dry cellar or the like at 50° to 55°F for 2 to 3 months.

Properly saved seeds should last for 6 years.

PUMPKINS NEED A LOT OF WATER: 1 INCH PER WEEK. AVOID GETTING THE FRUIT AND FOLIAGE WET, AS DAMPNESS INVITES ROT.

RADISHES

AS ANY GARDENER WILL TELL YOU, THE CYCLES OF NATURE
REQUIRE PATIENCE. . . . EVEN THE FAST-GROWING RADISH REQUIRES TIME.
–M. J. Ryan, personal change expert (b. 1952)

Radishes are hardy vegetables that are grown for their roots as well as their edible leaves. They can be planted multiple times in a growing season—in both spring and fall, but not at the height of summer's heat. (Heat may cause radishes to bolt.)

Otherwise, radishes are one of the easiest vegetables to grow.

PLANTING

Choose a sunny spot. If radishes are planted in shade—even if neighboring vegetable plants shade them—they put their energy into producing larger leaves.

Before planting, till the soil (roots do not grow well in compacted soil) and remove any rocks. If the soil is clay, mix in sand to loosen it and improve drainage. Mix in aged manure and/or compost or an all-purpose fertilizer (follow the package directions). Radishes do best in soil that's rich in organic matter.

Direct-sow seeds ½ to 1 inch deep and 1 inch apart in rows 12 inches apart 4 to 6 weeks before the last spring frost. Water seeds thoroughly, down to 6 inches deep. Keep seeds moist until sprouts appear.

Sow again, every 10 days or so, while weather is cool, for a continuous harvest in late spring and early summer.

WIT & WISDOM

- *For hoarseness, swallow slowly the juice of radishes.*
  —18th-century remedy
- *Got a mosquito bite? Apply radish juice to take away the sting and itching.*

ROTATE RADISHES, GROWING THEM IN THE SAME PLACE ONLY EVERY THIRD YEAR.

For a fall crop, sow seeds 4 to 6 weeks before the first fall frost.

CARE
Thin radishes to 2 inches apart when plants are 1 week old, by snipping greens off at the soil line. (Add to salads: Radish thinnings are edible!) Or, if thinnings have been carefully extracted with roots, leaves, and stem intact, replant them. Transplants might be a bit stressed, but they should recover.

Keep soil evenly moist but not waterlogged. Drip irrigation is ideal.

Mulch thinly around radishes to help to retain moisture in dry conditions.

Weed often; weeds will quickly crowd out radishes.

DISEASES/PESTS *(see pages 158–166)*
Cabbage root maggots, clubroot, flea beetles, white rust

HARVEST/STORAGE
Harvest some varieties as soon as 3 weeks after planting, when roots are approximately 1 inch in diameter. Pull out one as a test. Ready spring radishes deteriorate quickly; do not leave roots in the ground past maturity, as they will get tough. Winter radishes keep in the ground for a few weeks after they mature, if the weather is cool. Finish the harvest before frost.

Cut off the radish tops and tails and wash and dry the roots thoroughly. Store in plastic bags in the refrigerator. Radish greens can be stored separately in a plastic bag in the refrigerator for up to 3 days.

RECOMMENDED VARIETIES*
'Burpee White': spring variety; white skin

'Daikon': white, Japanese "winter radish"; up to 16 inches long; does best in cooler climates or during cooler portions of the growing season

'French Breakfast': late-maturing; can tolerate moderate heat

'Watermelon': white skin, pinkish center; mild, sweet taste

*Radishes such as 'Dragon's Tail' and 'Rat's Tail' are grown for their seedpods. Space 18 inches apart; harvest pods when pencil-thin.

RUTABAGA

WELL, RING-TAILED RUTABAGAS.
–Against the Day, *by Thomas Pynchon, American writer (b. 1937)*

Rutabagas, aka swedes, are biennial root vegetables usually grown annually for both their softball–size golden root and their greens.

Rutabagas are often confused with turnips. Both require similar care, but rutabagas take longer to reach maturity. Rutabaga's blue-green foliage is smooth and waxy, and the root usually has yellow flesh. Turnip roots are often pink and white and generally have white flesh.

Rutabaga is a cool-weather crop that tolerates frost and drought. It is primarily grown in the northern United States, Canada, and northern Europe.

PLANTING

Rutabagas prefer full sun (or light shade)

SOIL HIGH IN ORGANIC MATTER—AGED MANURE AND/OR COMPOST—MAY HAMPER GROWTH AND CROP QUALITY.

and tolerate most soils. Grow them in the ground or in raised beds with deep, loose soil. Avoid planting rutabagas and other cole crops in the same place more than once every 3 or 4 years.

Plant in early to midsummer; time them to harvest about 3 months later. Light frost improves the roots' quality and flavor but only in those that mature in fall. Do not plant in spring and wait to harvest in fall; roots will become woody and fibrous if overly mature.

Sow seeds when the soil reaches 40°F; optimum soil temperatures are 40° to 60°F. Plant seeds ½ of an inch deep, 2 inches apart, in rows 14 to 18 inches apart. Seeds germinate in 4 to 7 days.

Apply a balanced (10-10-10) fertilizer, half at planting and half about 4 weeks after planting.

After germination, thin to 6 inches apart.

CARE
Use floating row covers to protect from pests.

Water with 1 to 1½ inches per week and more as roots reach maturity.

Mulch to retain moisture and keep the soil cool.

Control weeds with frequent, shallow cultivation.

Sustained average temperatures of over 80°F might cause bolting.

DISEASES/PESTS *(see pages 158–166)*
Aphids, black rot, cabbage root maggots, clubroot, flea beetles, root-knot nematodes, white rust, wireworms

HARVEST/STORAGE
Harvest when roots are 2 to 3 inches in diameter and especially tender or wait until roots are 4 to 5 inches in diameter for best taste.

To store, cut off the foliage to within 1 inch of the crown. Rutabagas keep for about 4 months at just above freezing in an environment with 90 to 95 percent humidity.

RECOMMENDED VARIETIES
'American Purple Top' and 'Laurentian' both have a globe-shape root with purple crown and yellow flesh.

WIT & WISDOM
- *Rutabagas are known as "Hanovers" in some mid-Atlantic states and as "table turnips" in parts of Canada.*
- *Rutabagas were once carved like pumpkins to be jack-o'-lanterns.*

SPINACH

THE ANSWER ISN'T ANOTHER PILL.
THE ANSWER IS SPINACH.
–Bill Maher, American comedian (b. 1956)

Spinach, a super–cold-hardy vegetable, is a tender-leaf crop that can be planted in very early spring and in fall and winter.

Spinach has growing conditions and requirements similar to those of lettuce, but it is more versatile. It can be consumed raw or cooked. Spinach is higher in iron, calcium, and vitamins than most cultivated greens and is one of the best sources of vitamins A, B, and C.

PLANTING

Spinach requires 6 weeks of cool weather from seeding to harvest and tolerates full sun to light shade.

Prepare the soil about a week before planting by mixing in aged manure and/or compost. Alternatively, prepare the soil in late summer or early fall, when spinach can also be sown where winters are mild.

Seeds can be started indoors, but this is not recommended, as seedlings are difficult to transplant.

Sow seeds in early spring as soon as the ground warms to 40°F. (Cover the soil with black plastic to speed its warming.)

Sow seeds ½ of an inch deep every 2 inches and cover with ½ inch of soil. Plant in rows 12 to 18 inches apart or sprinkle over a wide row or bed.

Water to keep the soil constantly moist. Use row covers to maintain cool soil and deter pests.

SPINACH CAN BE GROWN INDOORS UNDER PROPER CONDITIONS, INCLUDING SUN OR GROW LIGHTS.

Sow every couple of weeks during early spring for continuous harvest. Common spinach can not thrive in midsummer. For a summer harvest, try Malabar or New Zealand spinach, two similar leafy greens.

To distract leaf miners, sow radish seeds in alternate rows; leaf miner damage to radish tops does not affect their root growth.

For a fall crop, re-sow in mid-August, when the soil is no warmer than 70°F.

For an early-spring harvest in the following year, northern gardeners can sow spinach just before cold weather arrives in fall and protect young plants with a cold frame or thick mulch through winter. When the soil temperature reaches 40°F in spring, remove the protection and water plants well.

CARE

When seedlings stand about 2 inches tall, thin to 3 to 4 inches apart.

Weed carefully; roots are shallow and easily damaged.

Water regularly and mulch to retain moisture.

When plants reach one-third of their growth, side-dress with a high-nitrogen fertilizer, as needed. Nutrient deficiencies may appear as yellow or pale leaves, stunted or distorted growth, a purpling or bronzing of leaves, leaves dropping early, or other symptoms.

DISEASES/PESTS (see pages 158–166)
Leaf miners; leaf spot, Cercospora;

RECOMMENDED VARIETIES

There are four main types of spinach suited for spring and fall plantings:

• Baby-leaf is tender, with small-leaves. 'Baby's Leaf' is good for containers; 'Catalina' is heat-tolerant and resistant to downy mildew.

• Savoy has curly, crinkled, dark-green leaves, e.g., 'Bloomsdale' (many strains).

• Semi-Savoy has slightly crinkled leaves and can be difficult to seed. 'Melody' is resistant to cucumber mosaic virus and downy mildew;

mildew-resistant 'Remington' will grow in spring, summer, or fall; 'Tyee' is resistant to downy mildew.

• Smooth- or flat-leaf has spade-shape leaves. 'Giant Noble' is an heirloom that is slow to bolt; 'Nordic IV' is bolt-resistant.

Malabar (*Basella alba*), a vine, and New Zealand (*Tetragonia tetragonoides*), a perennial, resemble common spinach; both are heat-tolerant.

WIT & WISDOM

- *Phenology, the study of signs, suggests planting spinach when crocuses are blooming.*
- *Scatter spinach seeds around emerging bulb foliage to have a leafy green crop at the ready to cover bare spots left by deadheaded spring flowers.*

mildew, downy; mosaic virus, cucumber (spinach blight); white rust

HARVEST/STORAGE

Harvest a few outer leaves from each plant (so that inner leaves can develop) when leaves reach desired size, or harvest the entire plant, cutting the stem at the base.

Be aware of day length and heat: Increasing daylight (about 14 hours or longer) and warmer seasonal temperatures can cause spinach to bolt (develop a large stalk with narrower leaves and buds/flowers/seeds), which turns leaf taste bitter. Pull the plant and use the leaves. Or try to slow the bolting: Pinch off the flower/seed heads, keep the soil moist, and provide shade.

YOU CAN INITIALLY HARVEST JUST THE OUTER LEAVES FROM EACH SPINACH PLANT, ALLOWING THE INNER LEAVES MORE TIME TO DEVELOP.

SQUASH, SUMMER AND WINTER

THE TROUBLE IS, YOU CAN NOT JUST GROW ONE ZUCCHINI.
MINUTES AFTER YOU PLANT A SINGLE SEED, HUNDREDS OF ZUCCHINI WILL
BARGE OUT OF THE GROUND AND SPRAWL AROUND THE GARDEN,
MENACING THE OTHER VEGETABLES. AT NIGHT, YOU WILL BE ABLE TO HEAR
THE GROUND QUAKE AS MORE AND MORE ZUCCHINI ERUPT.
—Dave Barry, American writer (b. 1947)

Squash, especially zucchini, are prolific producers. Each plant will produce several squash during peak season; typically, one or two zucchini plants will produce a "bumper" (unusually large) crop, leaving you to give the squash away to neighbors or bake lots of zucchini bread.

Squash are generally divided into two categories, based on harvest time and how they are used:

- **Summer squash** are harvested in the summer. Varieties include crookneck, straightneck (aka "yellow summer"), and zucchini.

- **Winter squash** are harvested in autumn, just before or after reaching maturity. At this time, the skin is inedible, but the squash have a relatively long shelf life (some varieties will keep through winter, hence the name "winter squash"). Winter squash varieties include acorn, butternut, Hubbard, pumpkin, and spaghetti.

Despite the great diversity of squash, most commonly grown cultivated varieties belong to one of three species: *Cucurbita pepo, C. moschata*, or *C. maxima*. Over several generations, these plants have been cultivated to produce fruit in all kinds of shapes, colors, and flavors.

WIT & WISDOM

- *The word "squash" derives from* askutasquash, *the Narragansett Native American word meaning "eaten raw or uncooked."*
- *So-called squash bees—*Peponapis *and* Xenoglossa—*are excellent* Cucurbita *pollinators and especially so for zucchini and butternut squash. Look for them among the flowers in the first few hours after sunrise.*

PLANTING

Before planting, mix aged manure and/or compost into the soil; squash produces better if well fed, in sun, and in soil that is moist (not soggy) and well-draining.

Start seeds in peat pots 2 to 4 weeks before the last spring frost date (squash seedlings do not always transplant well; handle the roots gently) or direct-sow when all danger of frost has passed and

WINTER SQUASH ARE VINING PLANTS THAT REQUIRE SUPPORT AND SPACE.

the air and soil are at least 60°F.

Sow seeds in level ground 1 inch deep and 2 to 3 feet apart. Or sow three or four seeds close together in small mounds (or hills; the soil is warmer off the ground) in rows 3 to 6 feet apart. Consider planting a few seeds in midsummer to avoid problems from squash vine borers and other early-season pests and diseases.

If necessary, use row covers or frame protection in cold climates for the first few weeks of spring.

CARE

Mulch to discourage weeds, retain moisture, and protect shallow roots.

Water thoroughly, frequently, and consistently, with at least 1 inch per week. Water diligently when fruit form and throughout their growth period. Misshapen squash result from inadequate water or fertilization.

When the first blooms appear, side-dress with a balanced fertilizer.

Poor pollination can result in squash flowers that do not bear fruit or bear small fruit. Most squash plants produce both male (these appear first, on long thin stalks) and female flowers (these have an immature fruit behind them). To fruit, pollen from male flowers must be transferred to the female flowers by bees—or by the gardener. Pollinate the female flowers manually with a cotton swab or add plants that attract bees near the squash.

DISEASES/PESTS *(see pages 158–166)*

Aphids; blossom-end rot; cucumber beetles; mildew, downy; mildew,

MOST SUMMER SQUASH
ARE BUSH VARIETIES,
WHICH TAKE UP LESS
SPACE, BUT WINTER
SQUASH ARE VINING
PLANTS THAT NEED
MORE ROOM.

powdery; mosaic virus, cucumber; squash bugs; squash vine borers; stinkbugs

HARVEST/STORAGE

Harvest summer squash when tender and a bit immature (e.g., as "baby" squash or when 6 to 8 inches long; oversize squash have little taste). Cut—do not break—fruit off the vine, leaving at least 1 inch of stem.

To slow production, harvest fruit when small and/or remove male flowers.

If the harvest is interrupted (say, by your vacation), remove large squash on your return to reduce demands on the plants for moisture and nutrients.

Complete the harvest before the first fall frost; summer squash is highly susceptible to frost and heat damage.

Fresh summer squash have a relatively short shelf life. Store in the refrigerator for up to 10 days.

Harvest winter squash when the vine leaves turn brown, the stems are drying, and the rind is deep in color and hard (if you can pierce the skin with a fingernail, it's not mature)—usually from late September through October.

Before storing winter squash, dip it into or wash with a low-concentration bleach rinse (½ cup bleach to 5 cups water) to sanitize the skin and eliminate bacteria. Air-dry the fruit.

Store in a cool (40° to 50°F), dark place with good circulation. Many varieties of winter squash will last for most of the winter; acorn will not keep for more than a few weeks. Occasionally rotate and look for signs of rot. Remove any squash that show signs of decay.

RECOMMENDED VARIETIES

Summer squash...

'Cashflow': cylindrical zucchini type

'Cocozella (di Napoli)': zucchini heirloom

'Horn of Plenty': yellow crookneck type

'Sunburst': pattypan/scallop type

'Tigress': zucchini type

Winter squash...

'Blue Hubbard': heirloom; stores well

'Buttercup': long vines, round fruit

'Delicata': bush type; tolerant of powdery mildew

'Tuffy': acorn type; five or six fruit per plant

'Waltham Butternut' (aka 'Butternut'): large, tan fruit; flavor improves with storage

**MY DREAM IS TO BECOME A FARMER. JUST A BOHEMIAN GUY
PULLING UP HIS OWN SWEET POTATOES FOR DINNER.**
–Lenny Kravitz, American musician (b. 1964)

Sweet potatoes are a root vegetable and member of the morning glory family. (Potatoes are in the nightshade family; the edible portion is a tuber.)

"Sweets" are commonly grown in southern regions because they require at least 4 months of warm weather. Northern gardens can have success with select varieties grown in raised beds that are mulched with black plastic.

Just a few plants can produce a generous harvest of this nutritious, relatively low-calorie vegetable, which can be stored longer than winter squash.

PLANTING

Sweet potatoes are typically grown from slips—sprouts grown from existing sweet potatoes. Slips are available at garden centers and nurseries and from local farmers. Or you can start your own. Here's one of multiple methods: In the fall, look for unblemished, smooth, organic sweet potatoes at the super- or farmers' market. (Inquire about the variety.)

Store the sweets in a cool (55°F), dark place until mid-April or about 90 days before the last spring frost. At this time, place the sweets in containers on top of 3 inches of light, organic, well-draining soil. Leave space between each sweet. Lightly cover with a few inches of additional soil. Water now and as needed to keep soil damp, not soggy. Maintain the soil and room at 75° to 80°F (use a heating mat, if necessary) in sunlight. In 4 to 6 weeks, the slips will be 6 to 12 inches long, with leaves and roots.

Meanwhile, in the permanent bed, till the soil to a depth of 8 to 10 inches and add compost, perlite, coconut coir, and/or peat moss to help retain moisture. Avoid adding animal manure, including pelleted chicken manure; it can result in spindly and/or stained roots. Cover soil with black plastic, if necessary, to warm it.

Remove the slips from the sweet potatoes, roots attached. (If no roots form, remove the slip and place it in water; roots will appear in 1 to 2 weeks.) If it is too soon to plant, stand the slips in potting mix or sand and keep it moist until planting time.

Harden off the slips over 1 to 2 weeks, exposing them to filtered sunlight. If you purchase slips, plant them as soon as conditions are right.

Plant the slips on a warm, overcast day, when the soil has reached 60°F. Break off the lower leaves, leaving only the top ones. Set the slips deep enough to cover the roots and the stem up to the leaves (sweets form on the nodes), 12 to 18 inches apart.

Water with a high-phosphorous liquid fertilizer and then water generously for 7 to 10 days.

CARE
Side-dress with 5-10-10 fertilizer 3 to 4 weeks after transplanting.

Weed regularly.

Water regularly. Deep watering in hot, dry periods helps to increase yields.

SWEET POTATOES ARE TYPICALLY GROWN FROM SLIPS—SPROUTS GROWN FROM EXISTING POTATOES.

WIT & WISDOM
• *Sweet potatoes are used in folk remedies to treat asthma, night blindness, and diarrhea.*
• *Not sweet potatoes, yams are related to grasses and lilies.*

> **HANDLE SWEET POTATOES CAREFULLY; THEY BRUISE EASILY.**

Do not prune vines; they should be vigorous.

Late in season, reduce watering to avoid cracking of the sweet's skin—a problem in storage.

DISEASES/PESTS *(see pages 158–166)*
Flea beetles, stem rot (Fusarium wilt), sweet potato scurf, white rust, whiteflies

HARVEST/CURING/STORAGE
Harvest when the leaves and ends of the vines start turning yellow or about 100 days from planting. Loosen soil around each plant (18 inches around, 4 to 6 inches deep) to avoid injuring the tubers. Cut away some of the vines. Pull up the plant's primary crown and/or dig up the tubers by hand.

Shake off excess dirt; do not wash the roots.

Complete harvesting by the first fall frost.

Curing gives sweets their sweet taste and allows a second skin to form over any scratches and bruises. To cure, store roots in a warm place (about 80°F) at high humidity (about 90 percent) for 10 to 14 days—for example, on a table outdoors in the shade. Arrange sweets so that they are not touching.

After curing, discard any bruised sweets, then wrap each one in newspaper. Carefully pack them in a wooden box or basket. Store in a root cellar, basement, or the like with high humidity at 55° to 60°F. They should last for about 6 months.

RECOMMENDED VARIETIES

The fastest-growing sweet potato varieties have orange flesh, but you might also consider varieties with white, yellow, or even purple flesh. Note that orange-flesh varieties cook up moist, white and yellow sweet potatoes become creamy, and purple sweets are dry and starchy.

'Beauregard': dark red roots, dark orange flesh; stores well; good for northern growers

'Bush Porto Rico': good for small gardens and for baking

'Centennial': carrot-color; stores well; good for northern growers

'Jewel' (aka 'Yellow Jewel'): copper-color skin, orange flesh; disease-resistant; stores well

'Stokes': purple color; cooks well in savory dishes and mashes

'Vardaman': bush type; blue/purple foliage, golden skin, reddish-orange flesh; stores well; good for small gardens

SWISS CHARD

WHO SAYS THAT VEGETABLES HAVE TO BE SERVED ON A PLATE?
WHO SAYS THAT FLOWERS CAN ONLY GO IN A VASE?
–Karen Bertelsen, Canadian blogger at The Art of Doing Stuff, *on using*
Swiss chard and other edible plant foliage in a bouquet

Swiss chard—or simply "chard" is a member of the beet family. It does well in both cool and warm weather. It is a nutritional superfood, high in vitamins A, C, and K as well as minerals, phytonutrients, and fiber— plus, its rainbow of colors are beautiful!

PLANTING

Before planting, mix aged manure and/ or compost into the soil, as well as 5-10-10 fertilizer.

To speed germination, soak seeds in water for 24 hours prior to planting.

Sow seeds ½ to 1 inch deep, 2 to 6 inches apart, in rows 18 inches apart 2 to 3 weeks before the last spring frost date.

Continue planting seeds at 10-day intervals for a month.

To grow (not merely start) indoors, soak seeds for 24 hours in water. Plant in rich soil in a container with drainage holes. Place the container in a sunny window. Water to keep the soil damp.

For a fall harvest, sow seeds about 40 days before the first fall frost date. (Many varieties will tolerate a light frost.)

WIT & WISDOM

● *Swiss chard is also known as leaf beet, seakale beet, silver beet, and spinach beet.*

● *Swiss chard originated in the Mediterranean region and is not native to Switzerland. It is "Swiss" because, legend has it, a Swiss botanist determined its scientific name.*

CARE

When plants are 3 to 4 inches tall, thin to 4 to 6 inches apart or 6 to 12 inches if plants are large. Use scissors to avoid disturbing nearby plant roots—and harvest the cuttings!

Water evenly, especially during dry spells.

Mulch to retain moisture and suppress weeds.

When plants are about 1 foot tall, cut leaves back to 3 to 5 inches to encourage new tender growth.

DISEASES/PESTS *(see pages 158–166)*

Aphids; leaf miners; leaf spot, Cercospora; slugs/snails

HARVEST/STORAGE

Begin to harvest when plants are 6 to 8 inches tall. Cut off outer leaves 1½ inches above the ground (avoid damaging the plant's center). Harvest regularly, and plants will produce continually.

To extend the harvest, lift the plant, with roots in the soil, and transfer to a container in a greenhouse. Maintain the temperature at around 50°F. Initially, the chard will appear limp, but it should rebound.

Store washed/rinsed Swiss chard in the refrigerator in ventilated plastic bags.

To use, draw a sharp knife along the ribs to separate the leaves. Cook the ribs like asparagus (steamed, roasted, sautéed). Use the leaves as greens.

RECOMMENDED VARIETIES

'Bright Lights': dark green leaves, multicolor stems; bolt-resistant but less frost-hardy

'Fordhook Giant': dark green leaves, white stems; compact plant

'Lucullus': green leaves, white stems; heat-tolerant

'Peppermint': green leaves, pink-and-white-stripe stems; bolt-resistant; good for containers

'Rainbow': red, pink, white, yellow, orange, and striped leaves and stems

'Rhubarb': dark green leaves, deep-red stems; sow after risk of frost has passed, or it may bolt

'Ruby Red': green leaves, bright-red stems; sow after risk of frost has passed, or it may bolt

WHEN OVERGROWN, SWISS CHARD LEAVES LOSE THEIR FLAVOR.

TOMATOES

IT'S DIFFICULT TO THINK ANYTHING BUT PLEASANT THOUGHTS
WHILE EATING A HOMEGROWN TOMATO.
–*Lewis Grizzard, American writer (1946–94)*

Let's hear it for America's favorite vegetable! Tomatoes are relatively easy to grow and come in a wide range of flavors. With proper care, any plant will produce a bumper crop.

In northern regions, tomato plants need at least 6 hours of sunlight daily; 8 to 10 hours are preferred. In southern regions, light afternoon shade (natural or applied, e.g., row covers) will help tomatoes to survive and thrive.

TOMATO TYPES

■ **Determinate,** better known as "bush," varieties grow 2 to 3 feet tall. These varieties tend to provide numerous ripe tomatoes at one time, do not put on much vegetative/leaf growth after setting fruit, and tend to fruit for a (relatively) brief period of time. They are generally less productive in the latter part of the growing season. Determinate tomatoes do not require staking or caging. These plants are ideal for containers and small spaces. Most paste tomatoes are determinate.

■ **Indeterminate,** better known as "vining," varieties produce the largest types of mid- to late-season slicing tomatoes all summer and until the

WIT & WISDOM

• To ease a headache, drink tomato juice blended with fresh basil.
• Biologically speaking, tomatoes are fruit, but in 1893, the U.S. Supreme Court ruled that they must be vegetables because they are most often served during the main part of a meal, either alone or with other vegetables.

first frost. Because indeterminates experience more vegetative/leaf growth, their production tends to be spread more evenly throughout the season. Indeterminate tomatoes need staking.

'GREEN ZEBRA' IS AN INDETERMINATE HEIRLOOM TOMATO.

These are ideal in large gardens. Most beefsteak and cherry tomatoes are indeterminate.

PLANTING

Start seeds indoors ½ of an inch deep 6 to 8 weeks before the last spring frost date.

Two weeks before transplanting, select a site with full sun where tomatoes (and members of their family, especially eggplants, peppers, and potatoes) have not grown in the previous couple of years. Dig soil to about 1 foot deep and mix in aged manure and/or compost.

Harden off seedlings for a week before transplanting. Set them outdoors in the shade for a few hours on the first day. Gradually increase this time each day to include some direct sunlight. Transplant after all danger of frost has passed and the soil is at least 60°F.

When planting seedlings, pinch off a few of the lower leaves. Here are two ways to set them into the soil:

1. Place each root ball deep enough such that the bottom leaves are just above the surface of the soil. Roots will grow all along the plant's stem underground. Plant seedlings 2 to 3 feet apart. Crowded plants will not get sufficient sun and the fruit may not ripen.

2. Alternatively, lay long, leggy transplants on their sides in trenches 3 to 4 inches deep. Bury the stems up to the first set of true leaves. Roots will develop along the buried stem. If you plant this way, consider setting four tomato plants in compass-point positions (north, south, east, west). This formation enables you to fertilize and water the plants in the middle.

TOMATOES COME IN A VARIETY OF COLORS AND SIZES, AS SHOWN BY
'BLACK KRIM' (LEFT) AND 'YELLOW MINI' (RIGHT).

Remember to allow enough space for the plants to spread out.

Tomato seeds can be direct-sown at a ½-inch depth—but not before the soil is at least 55°F. Note that 70°F soil is optimum for maximum germination within 5 days. Be certain that your growing season is long enough to bring the plants to maturity.

Place tomato stakes or cages in the soil at planting. Staking and caging keep developing fruit off the ground and help the plant to stay upright. Sprawling plants (with no support) can produce fine crops if you have the space and the weather cooperates.

Water well to reduce shock to the roots.

GROWING TOMATOES IN POTS

Use a large pot or container (at least 20 inches in diameter) with drainage holes and loose, well-draining soil (e.g., at least 12 inches of a good potting mix with added organic matter).

Choose bush or dwarf varieties. Many cherry tomatoes grow well in pots. Taller varieties may need to be staked.

Plant one tomato plant per pot and give each at least 6 hours of full sun per day.

Keep soil moist. Check daily and provide extra water during heat waves.

CARE

Water in the early morning so that plants have sufficient moisture to make it through a hot day. Water generously in the first few days and then with about 2 inches per week during the growing season. Deep watering encourages a strong root system. Avoid overhead and afternoon watering.

Mulch 5 weeks after transplanting to retain moisture, keep soil from splashing

between branches and the main stem). This aids air circulation and allows more sunlight into the middle of the plant.

Gently tie the stems to stakes with rags, nylon stockings, twine, or soft string.

As a plant grows, trim the lower leaves from the bottom 12 inches of the stem.

If no flowers form, plants may not be getting enough sun or water (too little can stop flowering). Flower drop-off could be due to high daytime temperatures (over 90°F). Provide shade during the hottest part of the day by using row covers or shade cloth.

If plants produce a lot of flowers but no fruit, the cause might be inadequate light, too little water or inconsistent watering, too cold or hot temperatures (above about 75°F at night/90°F during the day), or not enough pollinators. Low humidity can also affect pollination; the ideal is 40 to 70 percent. If humidity is low, mist the plant to help pollen to stick.

DISEASES/PESTS *(see pages 158–166)*
Anthracnose; aphids; blight, early; blight, late; blossom-end rot; Colorado potato beetles; corn earworms (aka tomato fruitworms); cracking; cutworms; flea beetles; Fusarium wilt; leaf miners; mildew, powdery; mosaic virus, cucumber; mosaic virus, tomato; root-knot nematodes; slugs/snails; stinkbugs; tomato hornworms; whiteflies

HARVEST/STORAGE
Leave tomatoes on the vine for as long as possible. Harvest red tomatoes when they are firm and very red, regardless of size, with perhaps some yellow remaining

THE OPTIONS ARE ALMOST ENDLESS WHEN IT COMES TO CHOOSING TOMATOES.

the lower leaves, and control weeds.

Side-dress with compost or liquid seaweed or fish emulsion every 2 weeks, starting when tomatoes are about 1 inch in diameter. Avoid high-nitrogen fertilizer unless plants have yellow leaves. Too much nitrogen will result in lush foliage but few flowers and little or no fruit. If plants have purple leaves, fertilize with phosphorus.

If growing vining tomatoes, pinch off suckers (new, tiny stems and leaves

BELOW 50°F, TOMATOES STOP RIPENING.

around the stem. Harvest tomatoes of other colors—orange, yellow, purple, or another rainbow shade—when they turn the correct color.

If temperatures start to drop and tomatoes—handpicked or dropped by the plant—are not ripening, use one of these methods:

1. Pull up the entire plant, brush off dirt, remove foliage, and hang the plant upside down in a basement or garage. Pick tomatoes as they ripen.

2. Place mature, pale green tomatoes, stem up, in a paper bag and loosely seal it. Or wrap them in newspaper and place in a cardboard box. Store in a cool (55° to 70°F), dark place. Cooler temperatures slow ripening; warmth speeds it. To hasten ripening, add an apple or banana to the bag or box. Check weekly and remove soft, spotted, diseased, or ripe fruit.

Never place tomatoes on a sunny windowsill to ripen; they may rot before they are ripe!

Never refrigerate fresh tomatoes. Doing so spoils the flavor and texture that gives them that garden tomato taste.

To freeze, core fresh unblemished tomatoes and place them whole in freezer bags or containers. Seal, label, and freeze. The skins will slip off when they thaw.

RECOMMENDED VARIETIES

Tomatoes grow in all sizes, from tiny "currant" to "cherry" to large "beefsteak." There are thousands of tomato varieties to suit different climates and tastes. Here are a few of our favorites.

Early varieties (fewer than 70 days to harvest) . . .

'Early Cascade': indeterminate; fruit in clusters; disease-resistant

'Early Girl': indeterminate; meaty fruit

Midseason varieties (70 to 80 days to harvest) . . .

'Fantastic': indeterminate; disease- and crack-resistant

'Floramerica': determinate; disease-resistant

Late-season varieties (more than 80 days to harvest) . . .

'Amish Paste': indeterminate heirloom; acorn-shape fruit

'Brandywine': indeterminate heirloom

Cherry tomatoes . . .

'Matt's Wild Cherry': indeterminate; disease-resistant (including blight)

'Sun Gold': indeterminate; apricot-color fruit on grapelike trusses; resistant to Fusarium wilt and tobacco mosaic virus

TURNIPS

ONE WHO IS PROUD OF ANCESTRY IS LIKE A TURNIP;
THERE IS NOTHING GOOD OF HIM BUT THAT WHICH IS UNDERGROUND.
—Samuel Butler, English writer (1835–1902)

Turnips are cool-weather vegetables that can be grown in spring and fall; they do not like the hot summer months. Note that an autumn crop, seeded in late summer, is usually sweeter and more tender than a spring crop—and pests are less of a problem.

Turnips germinate in only a few days. Within a month, their bright greens are ready for harvest, and within a second month, the swollen roots can be taken up. Try them as an alternative to potatoes.

PLANTING

As soon as the garden can be worked, loosen the soil to a depth of 12 to 15 inches. Mix in 2 to 4 inches of aged manure and/or compost. Add sand to heavy, clay soil to improve drainage.

Turnips grow best in full sun when temperatures range from 40° to 75°F. For a late spring harvest, sow seeds directly in the soil, ¼ to ½ of an inch deep, 1 inch apart, in rows 12 to 18 inches apart, 2 to 3 weeks before the last frost date. Turnip seedlings do not transplant well.

For an autumn harvest, sow seeds in late summer, after crops of onions, squash, beans, or sweet corn. For a later autumn harvest, sow seeds in early autumn.

Cover seeds with not more than ½ of an inch of soil.

Water well and consistently.

> **PROTECT SPRING CROPS FROM PESTS WITH ROW COVERS AT PLANTING.**

WIT & WISDOM

- *Turnips like a dry bed but a wet head.*
- *In 19th-century Ireland, Halloween jack-o'-lanterns were carved from turnips, not pumpkins. Lit by a candle inside, the grotesque faces were intended to scare away demons and evil spirits.*

CARE

When seedlings are 4 inches tall, thin to 4 to 6 inches apart. Crowding can result in small or malformed roots.

Weed regularly.

Mulch heavily to minimize weeds and retain moisture.

Water regularly to keep soil lightly moist; 1 inch per week should prevent roots from becoming tough and bitter.

Turnips are hardy biennials; they naturally flower and go to seed (bolt) in the second year. Bolting in the first year could be due to stress, such as caused by extreme temperatures (cold or hot) or lack of nutrients or water. Such stresses can also result in little or no root growth, a root that grows aboveground, or greens only.

DISEASES/PESTS *(see pages 158–166)*

Aphids; black rot; cabbage root maggots; clubroot; flea beetles; mildew, downy; mildew, powdery; stinkbugs; white rust

RECOMMENDED VARIETIES

If you are growing turnips primarily for greens, almost any turnip variety will do.

For roots, try these . . .

'Gold Ball': yellow skin; soft, yellow flesh; harvest at 3 inches in diameter for maximum sweetness (will grow to 4 to 5 inches)

'Golden Globe': roots with amber skin; firm, crisp, sweet flesh; tasty tops

'Just Right': pure white roots, delicious greens; extremely cold-tolerant; stores well; not recommended for a spring crop, as it tends to bolt early

'Purple Top White Globe': roots have purple shoulders, delectable leaves; heirloom

HARVEST/STORAGE

Harvest greens when small; leaves taste best when young and tender. Cut leaves 2 inches above the base; they may grow back. Harvest just a few at a time if also growing for roots.

Harvest roots at any size; however, small, young turnips are more tender.

The flavor of a fall crop improves—it sweetens—after one or a few light frosts.

Mulch to harvest later in the season and to protect from a hard freeze.

Store in a cool (32° to 38°F), dark place for up to 3 or 4 months or in the refrigerator for up to 2 weeks. To freeze, wash, cut into ½-inch cubes, blanch for 3 minutes, cool immediately in cold water, and drain. Pack into containers, label, and freeze.

HOW DOES MY GARDEN GROW?

VARIETY	SOURCE	YEAR PLANTED

HOW DOES MY GARDEN GROW?

VARIETY	SOURCE	YEAR PLANTED

GROWING CONCERNS

HOW TO FIGHT DISEASES AND PESTS

It's a rare gardener whose plot or pots are not visited by one or some of these vegetable villains. When this happens, learn from it, adapt, and prepare for next season. For more information about garden pests and diseases, go to Almanac.com/gardening/pests-and-diseases.

KEY WORDS

Bt: *Bacillus thuringiensis,* a natural bacterium that kills caterpillars and worms

Crop rotation: growing different crops in succession on the same land, which can discourage plant pests and diseases. See Crop Rotation, pages 192–194, for more information.

Handpick: to remove pests from a plant by hand and kill them. For example, you can pick beetles, bugs, caterpillars, worms, snails, and slugs off a plant using your hand or tweezers and drop them into a bucket of soapy water to drown them. Or you can crush pests and their eggs.

Soil solarization: a technique used to kill pests and diseases in the soil by covering the ground with clear plastic, in full sun, for 2 or so months in the summer before planting.

DISEASES

DISEASE	SIGNS	CONTROL/PREVENTION
Anthracnose: caused by several fungi	yellow/brown/purple/black spots on leaves; sunken, dark spots on stems and fruit; spots may develop a salmon-pink, gelatinous mass; eventually, rot; in corn, tops die back and stalks rot	destroy infected plants; choose resistant varieties; provide good drainage; avoid overhead watering; apply compost; use mulch; rotate crops
Black (Itersonilia) canker: caused by a fungus that prefers cool, wet conditions	shallow, reddish brown/purple/black cankers form on crown and/or shoulder of root crops; small, orange-brown spots on leaves may have green halos; flowers rot	choose resistant varieties; cover shoulders of root vegetables with soil; rotate crops
Black rot: caused by a bacterium that prefers warm, moist conditions; affects brassicas	yellow, V-shape areas on leaf edges that brown and progress toward leaf center; leaves eventually collapse; stem cross sections reveal blackened veins	destroy infected plants; choose resistant varieties; provide good drainage; remove plant debris; rotate crops

DISEASE	SIGNS	CONTROL/PREVENTION
Blight, early: caused by fungi that prefer warmth, humidity	leaves, beginning with lower ones, develop dark, concentric spots, often with yellow outer ring, and eventually die; fruit/tubers/stems also may be affected	destroy infected plants; choose resistant varieties; maintain proper soil fertility; ensure good air circulation; avoid overhead watering; water in morning; disinfect tools; rotate crops
Blight, late: caused by a fungus-like organism that spreads quickly in persistent cool to moderate, moist conditions	small, greenish gray, water-soaked spots on leaves that enlarge and turn brown, sometimes with yellow halo; white, fuzzy growth on leaf undersides; stems also affected; fruit rots; tubers develop reddish brown dry rot	destroy infected plants; choose resistant varieties and certified, disease-free seed potatoes; ensure good air circulation; avoid overhead watering; remove plant debris; rotate crops
Blossom-end rot: disorder caused by lack of calcium in fruit, often due to roots failing to obtain sufficient water and/or nutrients	dark, water-soaked spots on blossom end of fruit (opposite stem) may enlarge and become sunken and leathery	remove affected fruit; plant at proper soil temperature; water deeply and evenly; use mulch; maintain proper soil pH (around 6.5) and nutrient levels; avoid excessive nitrogen; provide good drainage; prevent root damage
Clubroot: caused by a fungus-like organism	wilted/stunted plants; yellow leaves; roots appear swollen/distorted	destroy infected plants; solarize soil; maintain soil pH of around 7.2; disinfect tools; rotate crops
Cracking: tomato disorder caused by (1) fruit growing too rapidly for skin to handle, due to uneven moisture or high nitrogen, or (2) skin expansion/contraction during fluctuating temperatures	from stem end, skin breaks radially or in concentric circles	choose resistant varieties; water consistently; use mulch; maintain good leaf cover of developing fruit
Fusarium crown rot (of asparagus): caused by long-lived fungi	yellow ferns; stunting; wilting; reddish brown spots on lower stems/crown/roots; rot	destroy infected plants; solarize soil; do not establish new bed where asparagus had been grown within past 5+ years; choose resistant varieties; disinfect tools; avoid overharvesting; maintain crown vigor

DISEASE	SIGNS	CONTROL/PREVENTION
Fusarium wilt: caused by long-lived fungi that prefer warm, dry conditions	plants wilt (sometimes on just one side) in daytime; leaves turn yellow (lower ones first); later, entire plant wilts/dies; stunting; stem cross section reveals brown discoloration	destroy infected plants; avoid excessive nitrogen; in acidic soils, raise pH to 7.0; choose resistant varieties; disinfect tools; rotate crops
Leaf spot, Cercospora: caused by a fungus that prefers warm/humid conditions, damp nights	many small brown spots with red-purple halos on leaves that enlarge and turn gray; centers of spots eventually fall out, leaving the halos	destroy infected plants; weed; avoid overhead watering; ensure good air circulation; rotate crops
Mildew, downy: caused by fungus-like organisms that prefer cool, moist conditions	yellow, angular spots on upper leaf surfaces that turn brown; white/purple/gray cottony growth on leaf undersides only; distorted leaves or corn tassels; defoliation	remove plant debris; choose resistant varieties; ensure good air circulation; avoid overhead watering
Mildew, powdery: caused by several fungi that prefer shade and dry/moderately warm days with humid/cool nights	typically, white spots on upper leaf surfaces expand to flour-like coating over entire leaves; foliage may yellow/die; distortion/stunting of leaves/flowers	destroy infected leaves or plants; choose resistant varieties; plant in full sun, if possible; ensure good air circulation; spray plants with 1 teaspoon baking soda dissolved in 1 quart water; destroy crop residue
Mosaic virus, bean common: caused by a virus that attacks beans; often spread by infected seed and aphids	leaves show green mottling (mosaic pattern) and may be distorted, blistered, curled downward; plants stunted	destroy infected plants; choose resistant varieties and certified virus-free seed; use row covers; disinfect tools; weed; control aphids
Mosaic virus, cucumber (aka "spinach blight" for spinach): virus that attacks many plants; often spread by aphids	varies with plant, but may include stunting, mottled green/yellow/white pattern or ringed spots on leaves/fruit; distorted leaf growth; warts on fruit	destroy infected plants; choose resistant varieties and certified virus-free seed; use row covers; disinfect tools; weed; control aphids; use mulch
Mosaic virus, lettuce: virus that attacks lettuce and other plants; often spread by infected seed and aphids	leaves may show green mottling (mosaic pattern) or brown spots and can be distorted, blistered, curled backward; plants stunted; heads may be distorted or fail to form	destroy infected plants; choose resistant varieties and certified virus-free seed; use row covers; disinfect tools; weed; control aphids

DISEASE	SIGNS	CONTROL/PREVENTION
Mosaic virus, tomato: virus often spread by infected seed/human activity/tobacco products (tobacco mosaic virus is closely related)	mottled, curled, distorted, or fernlike yellow/green leaves; plants stunted; fruit ripens unevenly and/or shows browning	destroy infected plants; choose resistant varieties and certified virus-free seed; avoid replanting in same location; wash hands before/after handling; disinfect tools; avoid using tobacco products nearby
Potato scab, common: caused by a bacteria-like organism	brown, rough, corky spots that can be shallow/raised/sunken	choose resistant varieties and certified disease-free potato seed; maintain soil pH between 5.0 and 5.2; dust seed potatoes with sulfur before planting; use pine needle mulch; keep soil moist after tubers start to form; do not use manure; rotate crops
Rust, asparagus: caused by a fungus that needs moisture to spread	pale green spots on emerging stalks become yellow/orange with concentric rings; in summer, reddish-brown blisters release rust-color spores that later turn black; brown ferns; defoliation; reduced vigor	destroy crop residue; choose resistant varieties; ensure good air circulation; avoid new plantings near established beds
Stem rot (aka Fusarium wilt of sweet potatoes): caused by long-lived fungi that prefer warm, dry conditions	yellow/puckered leaves; older leaves drop; wilting vines; plants eventually die; stems under-/near ground may appear slightly blue; stem cross section reveals brown/purple/black discoloration, especially near ground	destroy infected plants; choose certified, disease-free slips and resistant varieties; rotate crops
Sweet potato scurf: caused by a fungus that prefers humidity and soil that is wet/poorly drained or high in organic matter	skin-deep, dark brown/black spots or blotches on root tuber that may enlarge in storage; roots may shrivel; reduced shelf life	choose certified disease-free plants or use vine cuttings or sprouts cut at least 1 inch above soil line; disinfect tools and storage containers; rotate crops
White mold: caused by long-lived fungi that prefer cool, moist conditions; affects many plants	pale gray, "water-soaked" areas on stems, leaves, and other plant parts that enlarge and develop white, cottony growth, later with black particles; bleached areas; crowns/fruit rot; plants wilt/collapse	destroy infected plants; ensure good air circulation; water in morning; weed; destroy crop residue; rotating crops on 5-year or longer cycle may help

DISEASE	SIGNS	CONTROL/PREVENTION
White rot: caused by a long-lived fungus that prefers cool, moist conditions; affects alliums	leaves yellow, wilt, and die, starting with oldest; white, cottony growth at stem base or on bulb, later with black, poppy seed–like particles; roots rot	destroy infected plants; choose disease-free cloves/sets/transplants; destroy crop residue; disinfect tools; solarize soil; rotating crops on 5-year or longer cycle may help
White rust (aka white blister rust): caused by fungus-like organisms that prefer warm days and cool/moist nights	chalk-white blisters mainly on leaf undersides; small, yellow-green spots or blisters, sometimes in circular arrangement, on upper leaf surfaces; possible distortion or galls; flowers/stems may also be infected	destroy infected plants; choose resistant varieties; weed; destroy crop residue; rotate crops

PESTS

PEST	SIGNS	CONTROL/PREVENTION
Aphids: tiny, pear-shape, soft-bodied insects that suck sap from succulent/new growth	misshapen/yellow leaves; distorted flowers/fruit; sticky "honeydew" (excrement); sooty, black mold	grow companion plants; knock off with water spray; apply insecticidal soap; put banana or orange peels around plants; wipe leaves with a 1 to 2 percent solution of dish soap (no additives) and water every 2 to 3 days for 2 weeks; add native plants to invite beneficial insects
Asparagus beetles: two types, common (adults have six cream-color spots on a blue-black, oval body with red margins; gray larvae; dark brown eggs; both larvae and adults feed on asparagus ferns and spears) and spotted (adults have 12 dark spots on a red-orange body; orange larvae; green eggs; larvae feed on asparagus berries, adults on all parts)	spears turn brown and bend with a hook; defoliation; damaged fruit/seeds	handpick; remove plant debris; add native plants to invite beneficial insects
Cabbage loopers: smooth, white-striped, green caterpillars that move like inchworms become gray-brown moths with white "8" on each wing; yellow eggs	large, ragged holes in leaves from larval feeding; defoliation; stunted or bored heads; excrement	handpick; add native plants to invite beneficial insects; spray larvae with insecticidal soap or Bt; use row covers; remove plant debris

PEST	SIGNS	CONTROL/PREVENTION
Cabbage root maggots: white maggots become gray flies that resemble small houseflies	wilted/stunted plants; off-color leaves; larvae feeding on roots	use collars around seedling stems; monitor adults with yellow sticky traps; use row covers; destroy crop residue; till soil in fall; rotate crops
Cabbageworms, imported (aka cabbage whites, cabbage "moths"): slow-moving, velvety green caterpillars with thin, yellow stripe along back become black-tipped, white butterflies with two or three black spots on each wing	leaves have large, ragged holes or are skeletonized; heads bored; dark green excrement; yellowish eggs laid singly on leaf undersides	handpick; use row covers; add native plants to invite beneficial insects; grow companion plants (especially thyme); spray Bt
Carrot rust flies: small, cream-color maggots become tiny, red-headed, metallic-black flies with yellow legs	wilted/stunted plants; tunnels with rust-color excrement in roots of carrot-family crops; root rot	monitor adults with yellow sticky traps; use row covers; add native plants to invite beneficial insects; destroy crop residue; rotate crops
Colorado potato beetles: red-orange, humpback larvae with black spots become oval, yellow-orange beetles with 10 black stripes	yellow-orange eggs laid in clusters on leaf undersides; larvae and adults chew holes in foliage	handpick; use straw mulch; weed; use row covers; destroy crop residue; rotate crops
Corn earworms (aka tomato fruitworms): pale-headed, variably colored caterpillars with white and dark stripes and tiny black spines become moths that are usually yellowish brown	on corn, eaten silks and kernels; excrement; larvae also attack tomatoes and other plants, eating fruit/pods/leaves/flowers	remove larvae; apply mineral or vegetable oil to tips of corn ears; select corn varieties with tight husks; plant early; add native plants to invite beneficial insects; till soil in fall; spray Bt
Cucumber beetles: two common types, striped (yellow adults with three black stripes) and spotted (yellow-green adults with 12 spots); larvae are whitish grubs (spotted version aka "southern corn rootworms") that feed on roots; may transmit bacterial wilt	holes in leaves/flowers; rasped fruit; plants stunted/die (Bacterial wilt signs: wilting; plants die; ends of cut stems, when pressed together for 10 seconds and pulled apart, release stringy, white sap)	handpick; mulch heavily; use row covers; destroy plants infected with bacterial wilt
Cutworms: large caterpillars that curl into a "C" become gray/brown/black mottled moths; larvae of some species feed on upper parts or roots/tubers	wilting; severed stems of seedlings and transplants just above or below soil line; whole seedlings disappear	handpick; in spring before planting, cultivate soil to reduce larvae; wrap a 4-inch-wide collar made from cardboard or newspaper around each stem, sinking 2 inches into soil; weed; use row covers; destroy crop residue

PEST	SIGNS	CONTROL/PREVENTION
Earwigs, European: small, elongated, brown insects, with forceps at hind end; like moisture; active at night; also prey on garden pests	many small holes in leaves/flowers/fruit/ stems; corn silks eaten	trap in tuna can filled with 1/2 inch of fish oil and sunk in soil such that edge is slightly above ground level; remove plant debris
Flea beetles: soil-dwelling, thin, white grubs become tiny, shiny, black/ brown/bronze/gray beetles, some striped, that jump when disturbed	numerous tiny holes in leaves	use row covers; mulch heavily; add native plants to invite beneficial insects
Japanese beetles: C-shape, whitish grubs become copper-color beetles with metallic green heads that feed on a wide variety of plants	leaves skeletonized (only veins remain); stems/ flowers/fruit chewed; in corn, damage to husks/ kernels/silk; grubs feed on roots	handpick; use row covers; plant tansy near infested plants
Leaf miners: yellow/white maggots become tiny flies (often black with yellow)	meandering blisters in leaves caused by tunneling larvae	remove infested leaves; weed; use row covers; till soil early in season; rotate crops
Leafhoppers: pale, wingless nymphs mature to tiny green/brown/gray/ yellow/multicolor, wedge-shape adults; both stages suck sap and hop or run sideways when disturbed; adults fly; may transmit plant diseases	white shed skins on leaf undersides (from nymph molting); stippling (many tiny spots) on leaves; "hopperburn" (leaves yellow/brown, curled, or stunted); reduced yield	knock nymphs off leaf undersides with strong spray of water; use row covers; monitor adults with yellow sticky traps; weed; destroy crop residue
Mexican bean beetles: yellow, spiny grubs become adult beetles similar to ladybugs, but copper-color with 16 black spots; both stages feed on leaf undersides; check there for yellow egg clusters, too	"lacey," skeletonized foliage; dark holes on bean pods	handpick; purchase and release beneficial wasp *Pediobius foveolatus* when larvae observed; destroy severely infested plants; use row covers
Onion maggots: small, cream-color maggots become tiny, bristly, gray-brown flies with large wings; feed on alliums; prefer cool, wet weather	limp, yellow, or stunted plants; larvae feed on roots/bulbs/stems and may spread bacteria	use row covers; harvest on a timely basis; monitor adults with yellow sticky traps; weed, especially wild onions; destroy crop residue; rotate crops

PEST	SIGNS	CONTROL/PREVENTION
Root-knot nematodes: microscopic roundworms that feed on sap in roots of many plants; prefer warm soil temperatures	typically, roots "knotty" or galled; plants stunted/ yellow/wilted; root crops forked/pimpled	destroy crop residue, including roots; choose resistant varieties; solarize soil; add aged manure/ compost; disinfect tools; till in autumn; rotate crops
Slugs/snails: soft-body mollusks; snails protected by shell; both prefer cool/moist/shady conditions; active mostly at night or on cloudy/foggy days	irregular holes in leaves/ flowers; gouged fruit; slimy secretion on plants/soil; seedlings "disappear"	handpick; avoid thick bark mulch; use copper plant collars; avoid overhead watering; lay boards on soil in evening, and in morning dispose of "hiding" pests in hot, soapy water; drown in deep container filled with 1/2 inch of beer, or sugar water and yeast, and sunk so that top edge is slightly above ground; apply 1-inch-wide strip of food-grade diatomaceous earth as barrier
Squash bugs: small, green/gray, black-leg nymphs become large, dark gray/brown, flat-back adult bugs that often have orange and brown–striped edges; both suck plant sap from cucurbits; disperse quickly when disturbed; emit odor when crushed	many small, yellow/ brown/black spots on leaves; wilt; scarred fruit	handpick; crush yellow/bronze egg clusters on leaf undersides; lay boards on soil and check for pests underneath each morning; remove plant debris; use row covers; rotate crops
Squash vine borers: large, cream-color, wrinkled larvae become orange-red/ black, wasplike, daytime moths with olive-green front wings and clear hind wings; larvae bore into vines	vines wilt suddenly; plants die; mushy area and/or green to orange-yellow, sawdust-like excrement on/near base of plant stem	if detected early, slit infested stem lengthwise halfway to remove borer(s), then bury the cut in moist soil to encourage rooting; wrap seedling stems in aluminum foil collar; catch moths with yellow sticky traps; use row covers if no pests previously, but uncover before flowering; destroy crop residue; rotate crops
Stinkbugs (including harlequin bugs): bright-color (varies with species), oval, wingless nymphs mature to shield-shape green or brown bugs; both stages suck sap from buds/leaves/flowers/fruit/seeds of many plants; hide when disturbed	yellow/white blotches on leaves; scarred, dimpled, or distorted fruit/pods; shriveled seeds; eggs, often keg-shape, in clusters on leaf undersides	destroy crop residue; handpick (bugs emit odor, wear gloves); destroy eggs; spray nymphs with insecticidal soap; use row covers; weed; till soil in fall

PEST	SIGNS	CONTROL/PREVENTION
Thrips, onion: wingless, slender, white/green/yellow nymphs become tiny, fast-moving, slender, yellow/brown insects with fringed wings; both stages suck cell contents from many plants; prefer hot, dry conditions; may transmit viruses	leaves, especially in folds near base, have white patches or silver streaks; brown leaf tips; blistering/bronzing on cabbage leaves; brown streaks on cauliflower curds; bulbs/heads distorted or stunted; curling or scarring	remove plant debris; choose resistant varieties; add native plants to invite beneficial insects; use row covers; use straw mulch; monitor adults with yellow or white sticky traps; use sprinklers or other overhead watering
Tomato hornworms: huge, green caterpillars with eight V-shape stripes and black "horn" on hind end become large, mottled, gray-brown hawkmoths (aka sphinx moths) with orange-yellow markings that fly like hummingbirds; larvae feed on solanaceous plants; (tobacco hornworm larvae are similar, with red horn)	chewed leaves (initially toward top of plant); rapid defoliation; black/green excrement; gouged fruit	handpick (leave larvae that have white, ricelike cocoons, which house braconid wasp parasites); till soil in fall and spring; weed; add native plants to invite beneficial insects; grow dill as a trap crop or basil/marigolds as repellents; spray Bt
Whiteflies: tiny, often clear/green, wingless nymphs become small, flylike insects with white, waxy wings; all stages suck sap on leaf undersides; prefer warm weather	sticky "honeydew" (excrement); sooty, black mold; yellow/silver areas on leaves; wilted/stunted plants; distortion; adults fly if disturbed; some species transmit viruses	remove infested leaves/plants; use handheld vacuum to remove pests; spray water on leaf undersides in morning/evening to knock off pests; monitor adults with yellow sticky traps; spray with insecticidal soap; invite beneficial insects and hummingbirds with native plants; weed; use reflective mulch
Wireworms: jointed, hard-body, shiny, brown, wormlike larvae or yellow/white soft-body larvae become dark-color, elongated beetles; adults click when righting themselves; larvae feed underground; damage more prevalent in cool, moist conditions	seeds hollowed; seedlings severed; stunting/wilting; roots eaten; tubers/bulbs bored	trap by digging 2- to 4-inch-deep holes every 3 to 10 feet, fill with mix of germinating beans/corn/peas or potato sections as bait, cover with soil or a board, in 1 week uncover and kill collected wireworms; sow seeds in warm soil for quick germination; provide good drainage; remove plant debris; rotate crops

DISEASE AND PEST RECORD

DISEASE RECORD	PEST RECORD

DISEASE _____

CONTROL MEASURES _____

_____

_____

_____

DISEASE _____

CONTROL MEASURES _____

_____

_____

_____

DISEASE _____

CONTROL MEASURES _____

_____

_____

_____

DISEASE _____

CONTROL MEASURES _____

_____

_____

_____

DISEASE _____

CONTROL MEASURES _____

_____

_____

_____

PEST _____

CONTROL MEASURES _____

_____

_____

_____

PEST _____

CONTROL MEASURES _____

_____

_____

_____

PEST _____

CONTROL MEASURES _____

_____

_____

_____

PEST _____

CONTROL MEASURES _____

_____

_____

_____

PEST _____

CONTROL MEASURES _____

_____

_____

_____

HOW TO KEEP CRITTERS OUT

THE WORLD HAS DIFFERENT OWNERS AT SUNRISE. . . . EVEN YOUR OWN
GARDEN DOES NOT BELONG TO YOU. RABBITS AND BLACKBIRDS HAVE THE LAWNS;
A TORTOISESHELL CAT WHO NEVER APPEARS IN DAYTIME PATROLS THE BRICK WALLS,
AND A GOLDEN-TAILED PHEASANT GLINTS HIS WAY THROUGH THE IRIS SPEARS.
—Anne Morrow Lindbergh, American writer and aviator (1906–2001)

DEER

- String blinking outdoor Christmas tree lights around the perimeter of your garden. Keep them on from dusk to dawn.
- Put a transistor radio in your garden and keep it on all night. Switch stations when you think of it.
- Fold lengths of chicken wire into pleats. Lay this around garden beds. Deer do not like the unstable feel of the chicken wire under their feet.

MICE

- Mice dislike the smell of peppermint; spread it liberally where you suspect the critters.

MOLES

- Give them a dose of castor oil. Mix 3 parts castor oil to 1 part dish detergent. Use 4 tablespoons of the concoction in a gallon of water. Soak the tunnels and entrances with the mixture.
- Dip an ear of corn into roofing tar and place it into one of their tunnels. They don't like the smell of tar.
- Eliminate grubs in lawns.

RABBITS

- Place dried sulfur or wood ashes around the edge of your garden.
- Sprinkle blood meal around your crops after each rainfall.

RACCOONS

- Put a radio in your garden and leave it on all night.
- Hang clothes and shoes that

UNCOMMON CRITTER-PROOFING TRICKS

• Cut old garden hose into lengths long enough to resemble snakes. Place the pieces on the ground throughout your garden. Critters will mistake the hose segments for garden snakes and vacate your premises. For best results, periodically move the fake snakes.

• After pruning roses, cut the canes into 6-inch pieces. Place these on the ground around lettuce, greens, and other low-growing, soft plants that rabbits, squirrels, and chipmunks enjoy. Note that this is effective in deterring small ground rodents but is useless in discouraging larger mammals such as deer.

smell of human perspiration around your garden or corn patch.

SKUNKS
- Put a radio in your garden and leave it on all night.
- Add motion-sensor lighting.
- Eliminate grubs in lawns.
- Prevent access to pet food, birdseed, and garbage.

SQUIRRELS
- Protect your garden with a wire fence buried about a foot into the ground so that squirrels can't dig under it.
- Lay aluminum foil across the top of vegetable pots; poke holes for water. Squirrels do not like the shiny reflection.
- Plant nasturtiums, marigolds, and mustard as a border around your vegetable garden; these plants have an unpleasant aroma.
- Sprinkle blood meal on the garden soil.
- Sprinkle cayenne pepper, pepper flakes, and/or garlic pepper on and around your plants when they are ready to bloom. Squirrels won't eat anything with cayenne.
- Get some mousetraps. Anchor them solidly to the ground in the area where the squirrels have been digging. Cover them with newspaper and sprinkle a little dirt on top. When a squirrel comes to dig, it will set off the traps. As the mechanism snaps, it will scare and throw dirt at the squirrel. Once it's scared enough times, it will find another digging area. Be sure to anchor the traps just in case the wind blows the newspaper off them. If the trap is anchored, the squirrel will not get hurt.

WOODCHUCKS
- Sprinkle blood meal or talcum powder around the perimeter of the garden.
- Plant a line of garlic near the woodchuck's entrance to the garden.
- Scatter hair clippings around the edge of the garden.

WATER WAYS

WATER IS THE DRIVING FORCE OF ALL NATURE.
–Leonardo da Vinci, Italian artist (1452–1519)

According to some experts, less is often more when it comes to watering vegetable crops. In areas without drought, a common mistake that new gardeners make is watering too much! There are methods and practices that can result in using less water but achieving better results with your plants.

START WITH GOOD SOIL

The best garden results start with good soil. See the chapters on soil types, soil testing, and the basics of amending your soil. Soils that are rich in organic matter absorb and retain moisture better.

CULTIVATE YOUR CROPS

Farmers and gardeners have long practiced regular cultivation. Moderation is key, however, as while cultivation can disrupt the upward "wicking" and subsequent evaporation of deep moisture, it can also add to overall evaporation by increasing the soil's surface area. But aerating the upper layer of soil does greatly improve the capture and retention of rainfall. Plus, it disrupts the germination and growth of weeds that would compete with crops for water.

A rototiller or push cultivator is good for large beds, but hand tools work fine in small plots. Alternate between fluffing up only the top 1 to 2 inches of soil and tilling down 5 or 6 inches— always being careful not to disturb crop roots!

Cultivate your garden early and often. After starting with bare ground, cultivate crops early in season and until plants become established; this will keep the soil well oxygenated.

Many gardeners stop cultivating their gardens in midsummer once crops are mature enough to outcompete weeds. But midsummer is the hottest time of year, when soil and plants are most vulnerable to moisture

A VOICE OF EXPERIENCE

One side of my house is narrow. I use that area for all of my pots that are growing stuff. I have also lined up rain barrels and heavy-duty trash barrels to collect the runoff from the roof, as there are no gutters on that side. I invert the trash can lids and poke several holes in the center so that the water can drain into each rubber barrel. Sure does help keep stuff watered, with the best possible water.

–T Anne, on Almanac.com

losses through evaporation and transpiration. Also, midsummer rains often come fast and furious, in the form of violent cloudbursts that drop a lot of rain in a short time. Frequent cultivation prepares your plots for dramatic percolation, allowing you to capture as much of this rainfall as possible, rather than have it run off or just puddle on the ground.

After a rainfall, stay off (do not step into) freshly cultivated soil for 3 days. This will prevent soil compaction and allow the rainwater to percolate down to the lower

root zone. You want plants to root deeply so that they do not become dependent on surface watering.

MULCH TO MINIMIZE THE NEED

Mulching complements cultivation. It is perhaps the #1 water-conserving technique for areas that receive less than 40 inches of rainfall annually. Organic mulches reduce evaporative moisture losses from the soil

surface, and, because the soil stays cooler, they also reduce transpiration water losses.

The best mulches are compost and other organic matter, which help to feed the plants as they grow. Lay mulches at least 2 inches thick onto moist soil and keep them topped up throughout summer.

If you are growing vining crops—cucumbers, melons, squashes—apply mulch when the plants begin to set runners. With fruiting crops such as tomatoes and peppers, wait until the blossoms drop and the plants begin to set their main crop, then mulch.

LOSE ANY GUILT ABOUT WILT

Temporary wilting during the heat of midday does not mean that a plant needs water. Some plants go through an obvious midday slump, which is an indication of the plant's natural adaptation to its environment. Visit your garden again in the early evening and see if the wilted plants have regained some turgidity. If they have come back—that is, if they look perkier—do not water.

Do not pamper your crops; plants are highly adaptable. They have the ability to draw water from deep in the soil. Periodically, take a trowel and dig down several inches into the zone where the roots are most active. If the soil is moist, there would be no benefit from watering.

BE WATER WISE

A healthy plant is one with deep root penetration. This occurs only if there is water deep in the soil.

Give your crops a good start. Saturate each plant hole when you transplant seedlings. When you water, saturate the soil enough that the moisture percolates down

SQUASH YOUR FEARS: YOU CAN BE A GARDENER!
DISCOVER PLANT GUIDES ON 📌 @ALMANAC

SOAKER HOSES VS. DRIP LINES

Soaker hoses are made of a porous material that allows water to slowly seep through it. Drip irrigation uses flexible tubing with tiny outlets called emitters that slowly drip water into the soil. Both are less wasteful than sprinklers.

After laying out the tubing or hoses in your garden, cover both systems with 2 inches of an organic mulch or use landscape fabric or plastic mulch. An inch of water slowly dripped onto the soil over a 6-hour period will soak in and not run off. Dig into the soil an hour after watering to see how deep the moisture went. Adjust the flow and timing accordingly. Once you have figured out the watering schedule for your garden, use a timer—and override it when rain is coming.

several inches.

Believe it or not, the best time to water can be during or immediately after a rainfall, especially one of ½ inch or so. By watering at that time, you can add sufficient water to ensure penetration down to 5 to 6 inches. If you wait a day or two, you will add only surface water, which evaporates rapidly.

With only frequent, light watering (or rain showers), your garden will never build a up a reserve of water in the soil.

So, cultivate, mulch, and water in the rain. And learn from nature: Spend more time observing your garden and less time watering.

FIVE SMART WAYS TO WATER

1. Water only when you need to. If you're not sure that your plants need water, check the soil moisture by digging a small hole with a trowel or with your finger. If the soil is cool and damp below the surface, leave watering for another time.

2. Water in the A.M. Watering early in the morning gives

MEASURING STICK TRICKS

A rain gauge or bucket—even a clean, empty tuna or vegetable can—can catch and measure how much rain or irrigation water your garden is getting and how long it takes Mother Nature or your watering system to drop an inch of water. Measure the water by putting a ruler into the container.

crops enough time to take up the moisture before it evaporates in the heat of the afternoon. Water-splashed foliage will also have time to dry before nightfall, minimizing problems with slugs and diseases.

3. Water where it matters. Direct the flow of water at the base of plants and avoid splashing the leaves. Water generously. A lot of water occasionally is better than little and often and will help to develop a better root system.

4. Water slowly. Sink plastic plant pots (with holes in the bottom) up to the rim next to thirsty plants such as squashes, then direct water into the pots. The water will be delivered directly to the root zone instead of running off the surface. Or, instead, remove the cap and cut off the bottom of a soda bottle. Set it into the soil, neck down, and fill with water.

5. Harvest water. Collect water off the roof of your house, shed, and/or greenhouse into water barrels. Locate the barrels close to where you need the water. Link multiple barrels to maximize storage; check local collection laws before buying equipment. Turn page for *How Much Water Is Enough?*

HOW MUCH WATER IS ENOUGH?

Here's a guide to help you estimate when and how much to water, assuming rich, well-balanced soil and little to no rainfall. Increase frequency during hot, very dry periods.

WATERING FORMULA: 1 INCH OF WATER PER 1 SQUARE FOOT PER WEEK = .62 GALLON

VEGETABLE	CRITICAL TIMES TO WATER	GALLONS OF WATER NEEDED FOR A 5-FOOT ROW	COMMENTS
Beans	When flowers form and during pod-forming and picking.	6 per week	Dry soil when pods are forming will adversely affect quantity and quality.
Beets	Before soil gets bone-dry.	3 per week	Water sparingly during early stages to prevent foliage from becoming too lush at the expense of the roots; increase water when round roots form.
Broccoli	Continuously for 4 weeks after transplanting.	3–5 per week	Best crop will result from no water shortage.
Brussels sprouts	Continuously for 4 weeks after transplanting.	3–5 per week	Plants can endure dry conditions once they are established. Give 6 gallons the last 2 weeks before harvest for most succulent crop.
Cabbage	Frequently in dry weather.	6 per week	If crop suffers some dry weather, focus efforts on providing 6 gallons 2 weeks before harvest. (Too much water will cause heads to crack.)
Carrots	Before soil gets bone-dry.	3 per week at early stage; 6 per week as roots mature	Roots may split if crop is watered after soil has become too dry.
Cauliflower	Frequently.	6 per week	Give 6 gallons before harvest for best crop.
Celery	Frequently.	At least 6 per week	If conditions are very dry, water daily.
Corn	When tassels form and when cobs swell.	6 per week	Cob size will be smaller if plants do not receive water when ears are forming.
Cucumbers	Frequently.	At least 3 per week	Water diligently when fruit form and throughout growth; give highest watering priority.

VEGETABLE	CRITICAL TIMES TO WATER	GALLONS OF WATER NEEDED FOR A 5-FOOT ROW	COMMENTS
Lettuce/ Spinach	Frequently.	2 per week	Best crop will result from no water shortage.
Onions	In early stage to get plants going.	3 per week	Withhold water from bulb onions at later growth stages to improve storage qualities; water salad onions anytime soil is very dry.
Parsnips	Before soil gets bone-dry.	Not more than 3 per week	Water only when very dry to keep plants growing steadily. Too much water will encourage lush foliage and small roots.
Peas	When flowers form and during pod-forming and picking.	3 per week	To reduce excess foliage and stem growth, do not water young seedlings unless wilting.
Peppers	Need a steady supply.	3–6 per week	Even moisture yields best performance.
Potatoes	When the size of marbles.	3–6 per week	In dry weather, give 6 gallons throughout the growing season every 10 days. Swings from very dry to very wet produce oddly shaped and cracked tubers.
Radishes	Need plentiful, consistent moisture.	3–6 per week	Keep soil moist for best quality.
Squashes	Frequently.	At least 3 per week	Water all types diligently throughout growth and when fruit form; give highest watering priority.
Tomatoes	For 3 to 4 weeks after transplanting and when flowers and fruit form.	6 per week	Frequent watering may increase yield but adversely affect flavor.

FACTS ABOUT FERTILIZERS

FERTILIZER DOES NO GOOD IN A HEAP, BUT
A LITTLE SPREAD AROUND WORKS MIRACLES ALL OVER.
–Richard Brinsley Sheridan, Irish writer (1751–1816)

For many gardeners, fertilizer is a mystery ingredient that can work wonders or, if applied improperly, wreak havoc. Here's how to eliminate the guesswork and grow better.

Remember that fertilizer is not plant food. Plants make their own food by photosynthesizing. Fertilizer provides supplemental elements that are often lacking in the soil. Think of fertilizer as vitamins.

Keep in mind that not all plants require fertilizer. There are six primary nutrients that plants require—carbon, hydrogen, oxygen, nitrogen, phosphorus, and potassium. The last three nutrients come from the soil. If the soil in which a plant lives is rich in nutrients and the microbial life that aids in the plant's uptake of these nutrients, then adding more can disturb that healthy ecosystem.

ORGANIC VS. SYNTHETIC FERTILIZERS

Organic fertilizers . . .
- come from and contain ingredients such as manure, blood meal, cottonseed meal, feather meal, crab meal, and so forth. (Not all products labeled "natural" are organic. Greensand, derived from inorganic mineral-based or "rock" matter, is an example of a natural, although inorganic, material.)
- work with soil microbes that break down fertilizers for a plant to absorb.

GOING TO THE BEACH?

Gather some seaweed. Plowed directly into the land or composted, seaweed makes excellent fertilizer and improves the physical character of the soil. It can also be used for top dressing.

- do not add excess salts and acid to the soil; they encourage healthy soil biology rich in microbial activity.

Synthetic fertilizers . . .
- are made in labs and derived from compounds like ammonium nitrate, ammonium phosphate, superphosphate, and potassium sulfate.
- speed plant growth and can enhance the bloom rate in flowering plants.
- are high in salts and can be detrimental to beneficial microorganisms.
- can "burn" foliage and damage plants when applied too heavily.
- boost plants but do little to improve the soil's long-term health, texture, or fertility.
- are highly water-soluble and leach out into streams and ponds.

In general, organic fertilizers need time to

enrich the soil (they are not "immediately available"); they are best applied in the fall so that the nutrients will be available in the spring. Some organically based fertilizers suited for spring application contain small amounts of synthetic fertilizers to ensure the immediate availability of nutrients. You may notice that the N-P-K ratio (listed on the packaging) of organic fertilizers is lower than that of synthetic fertilizers. By law, the ratio label can list only the nutrients that are immediately available.

GRANULAR VS. SOLUBLE FERTILIZERS

Granular fertilizers are solids that must be worked into the soil. They must be given time (and water) for dissolving to become available to plants. Slow-release fertilizers are a subset of granular formulations. A portion of the fertilizer is not immediately available to the plant. Nutrients are metered out over several weeks. Therefore, they are applied less frequently.

Sometimes called "liquid feed," **soluble fertilizers** are sold as ready-to-use solutions or packaged dry-milled materials that need to be dissolved in water. These tend to be quick-release fertilizers that are high in nitrogen and result in fast green growth.

To build the long-term health and fertility of soil, we recommend using granular organic fertilizers. Supplementing with an additional water-soluble

IF WE CAN OBTAIN VALUABLE MANURE FOR NOTHING BUT
THE LABOR, IT IS BETTER THAN PUTTING OUR HANDS INTO OUR POCKETS AND
PAYING 6 OR 8 DOLLARS AN ACRE FOR ARTIFICIAL MANURE.
–The New England Farmer, *1849*

fertilizer is a way to ensure that your plants have the nutrients that they need when they need a boost (during active growth).

OTHER NUTRIENTS

Much attention is paid to N-P-K (see page 28), but other key nutrients are needed for overall plant health. Soil test results may come with recommendations for adding the following trace minerals to the soil if they are found to be deficient.

Calcium (Ca) improves general plant vigor and promotes the growth of young roots and shoots.

Magnesium (Mg) regulates the nutrient uptake, aids in seed formation, and contributes to the dark green color of leaves, which is important for photosynthesis.

Sulfur (S) helps to maintain leaves' dark green color, encouraging vigorous plant growth.

GIVE PEAS A CHANCE!
POST PICS ON 📷. TAG US:
@THEOLDFARMERSALMANAC

PLANT SUPPLEMENTS

Plants can also get "vitamins" and nutrients from these soil amendments:

Alfalfa meal is a source of readily available nitrogen for plant growth and also feeds soil organisms. It contains vitamins, folic acid, and trace minerals.

Blood meal is very high in fast-release nitrogen. It also repels deer.

Fish meal, a by-product of fish farming, is an excellent source of nitrogen and potassium.

Kelp meal—dried, ground-up seaweed—provides trace minerals, amino acids, and enzymes that stimulate plant

and root growth and are beneficial to microbial life. By improving soil structure, it can help soil to hold moisture and reduce the effects of drought and frost.

Soybean meal contains high amounts of nitrogen and potassium that are released slowly as it breaks down. Look for organic sources; most commercially grown soybeans are genetically modified.

FERTILIZER TEA TIME!

You can save money by making effective fertilizers from plants in your garden. It's easy—just allow time for the tea to "steep."

Comfrey leaves have long been valued as natural fertilizer because they contain nitrogen and potassium, as well as several trace elements, which are released as the leaves decay. (Note that, on contact, the leaves can cause skin irritation.) The variety 'Bocking 14' (a cultivar of Russian comfrey) is preferred because it does not self-seed and may be slightly higher in nutrients than true comfrey.

The leaves of nettle, aka "stinging nettle," are high in nitrogen.

Here's how to make the tea: Harvest a large bag of comfrey or nettle leaves (wear gloves when handling either plant).

Squash the leaves in a large container, preferably with

HOW TO GROW STINGING NETTLE

Called "stinging" because of the intense burning or itching sensation felt when the plant's tiny hairs on leaves and stems make contact with skin, this perennial thrives in loose, moist, fertile soil in shade or (more vigorously) in sun. It can be grown from seed and by division. It enjoys a rapid growth rate—as much as 3 to 9 feet per year. Grow it in a pot, in a spot separate from other plants, or use barriers to limit or control spreading.

HOW TO GROW COMFREY

Comfrey (aka blackwort), a member of the borage family, is a perennial that requires average, well-draining soil. It will thrive in full sun (but prefers partial shade) and can be grown from seed or by division (best done in spring). The true ("common") variety readily and aggressively self-sows. Stems can reach to 5 feet in height (staking can reduce sprawl) and plants spread 2 to 6 feet. Each variety produces flowers; the colors range from blue/violet, yellow, and pink to white. Deadhead flowers to stop self-seeding and plant in a pot or use other barriers to limit or control the spreading of its deep-setting roots. At the end of season, cut the plant to the ground.

COMPANIONABLE COMFREY

When applied directly, comfrey leaves have almost magical powers:

• Throughout the season or at the end, bruise or roughly chop the stems and leaves and add them to the compost pile; they stimulate decomposition.

• Growing potatoes? Line the potato trench with comfrey leaves and cover with a sprinkling of soil before setting seed spuds. The leaves will decompose and serve as a potassium-rich fertilizer. (See page 125.)

• Repeat as above (for potatoes) if you are growing runner (aka butter) beans. (See page 71.)

• Boost any plant by burying layers of comfrey leaves about 2 inches in the soil. As the leaves decay, they will provide nutrients and help to control weeds.

a lid (to contain the smell, especially of comfrey).

Weigh down the leaves with a brick or rock and set the container aside for 1 to 2 weeks.

Pour off the liquid into a clearly labeled container. (Keep this container out of the reach of children.) To use, dilute 15 parts rainwater to 1 part comfrey.

Use a watering can when distributing the fertilizer. When watering, aim toward the soil and not the foliage, as fertilizers can cause leaf burn.

HOW TO MAKE COMPOST TEA

Compost tea is a liquid produced by extracting beneficial microorganisms (microbes)—bacteria, fungi, protozoa, nematodes, and micro arthropods—from compost by using a brewing process. A true compost tea contains all of the organisms that were present in the compost before brewing. The brewed water extract should also have soluble nutrients from the compost.

Compost tea can be made without aeration, although for best results, it is recommended. This recipe makes a batch for vegetable crops.

You will need . . .

1 brewing bag (can be fashioned from mesh material such as row cover and tied with twine; it should hold 5 to 6 pounds of dry ingredients)
1 5-gallon bucket, filled with water (let it sit for 24 hours to allow any chlorine to evaporate)
1 fish tank aerator
1 aquarium thermometer

Ingredients

1 large handful of compost
1 handful of garden soil
2 handfuls of straw
3 to 5 leaves from a healthy plant
1 cup fish hydrolysate (pulverized fish)*
1 cup seaweed extract*

*available at most garden centers

Put the compost, soil, straw, and leaves into the brewing bag, tie it tightly, and submerge it in the water. Add the fish hydrolysate and seaweed extract directly to the water. Place the aerator in the bucket and turn it on. Brew the tea for about 36 hours, monitoring the temperature; the optimal range is between 68° and 72°F.

Use the tea immediately after brewing; the longer it sits, the less active and effective it will be. To use, dilute the tea in a 3:1 water-to-tea ratio. Fill a backpack sprayer or spray bottle. Apply the tea in early morning or late evening to avoid burning leaves in the midday sun.

Monitor your brewing conditions. With each new batch, take note of the following . . .

■ **Brewing temperature.** If you are unable to reach the optimal range, consider buying a small, submersible aquarium heater, available at most pet stores.

■ **Microbial foods** (and quantities) added to the brew (for future reference).

IN . . .	USE AGED MANURE FROM . . .	ON . . .
Spring	Poultry	Vegetable gardens
Spring and summer (when crops are up)	Sheep	Vegetables (as top dressing)
Spring and fall	Cows, hogs, horses, poultry	Vegetable gardens
Fall	Cows, horses	Potato or root crop bed

■ **Brewing time.** If necessary, increase it to be effective.

Clean your equipment—the sprayer, the tank—well (hydrogen peroxide or ammonia is suitable) between each brew. Dirty equipment can breed harmful bacteria.

ANIMAL MANURE

As all-around fertilizer, barnyard or stable manure—often free from farmers and stables, if you haul it away—is a good source of organic matter and nutrients. Never use it fresh, when it is too "hot," or raw, and could burn plants. Use only aged or composted animal manure.

Horse manure ferments easily, but in the process it loses much of its nitrogen in the form of ammonia. To slow fermentation, keep the pile wet or mix it with aged cow or hog manure. To kill any "hot" (active) weed seeds, compost it before using.

Cow manure contains more water than horse manure and has the lowest value as plant food and fertilizer.

Hog manure ferments slowly and, because it comes from a diet that tends to be richer than that of horses and cows, is of high value.

Sheep manure is drier and richer than any other except that of poultry. Sheep chew

WHEN TO FERTILIZE	
Asparagus	Before growth starts in spring
Beans	After heavy bloom and set of pods
Beets	At time of planting
Broccoli	3 weeks after transplanting
Brussels sprouts	3 weeks after transplanting
Cabbage	2 weeks after transplanting
Carrots	5 to 6 weeks after sowing
Cauliflower	3 to 4 weeks after transplanting
Celery	At time of transplanting, and after 2 months
Corn	When 8 to 10 inches tall, and when first silk appears
Cucumbers	1 week after bloom, and every 3 weeks thereafter
Eggplant	At time of planting, and then every 2 weeks
Kale	When plants are one-third grown
Lettuce	3 weeks after transplanting
Onion sets	At time of planting, and then every 2 weeks until bulbing begins
Parsnips	1 year before planting
Peas	After heavy bloom and set of pods
Peppers	At time of planting, and after first fruit-set
Potato tubers	At bloom time or time of second hilling
Pumpkins	Just before vines start to run, when plants are about 1 foot tall
Radishes	Before spring planting
Spinach	When plants are one-third grown
Squash	When first blooms appear
Tomatoes	When fruit are 1 inch in diameter, and then every 2 weeks

their cud so finely that there are no weed seeds being inadvertently applied to the garden bed.

Poultry manure, the richest of the barnyard, is high in nitrogen and ferments easily. Always compost it before using.

GREEN MANURE, OR COVER CROPS

"Green manure" is the product of a variety of fast-growing ground-cover crops. It is an age-old technique— and a little goes a long way: When turned into the soil, cover crops can add the equivalent of 9 to 13 tons of fresh manure per acre, according to researchers at the Woods End Agricultural Institute in Mt. Vernon, Maine. No matter where you live or the size of your garden, you can grow cover crops.

The most common cover crops are legumes and grasses; brassicas are another option.

Legumes thrive and maximize their ability to store, or fix, nitrogen if they are inoculated with beneficial bacteria called rhizobia (of the genus *Rhizobium*). Purchase seeds described as "rhizocoated" or inoculate the seeds yourself: Shake dampened seeds in a container with the powdered inoculant until they are covered or, if you are planting by hand, sprinkle a small amount of inoculant into the

WHEN TO GO GREEN

In northern areas, cover crops are usually planted in late summer or early fall, after most vegetables have been harvested but before snow. Clear away any debris and weeds. Rake the bed smooth. Add any soil amendments. Broadcast the cover crop seed by hand, rake it in, and tamp down the soil with a roller or the back of the rake. If no rain is expected, water.

In the South, cover crops can be planted anytime there is a bare spot in the garden.

seed hole, set the seed, and cover it with soil immediately. Heat and sunshine will kill the beneficial bacteria. Each legume requires specific bacteria, so buy the correct match.

For fixing nitrogen, the best legumes are alfalfa, cowpeas, and hairy vetch. Other legumes are clovers, field peas, fava beans, lupine, trefoil, lespedeza, peas, snap beans, soybeans, and woolly pod vetch. Some of these crops, such as the beans and peas, give twice: They produce a harvest before being turned into the soil. (Peas, rotated every year, help to spread

nitrogen in a small garden.)

Green grasses and grains are fast-growing crops that can be planted in season. Buckwheat may be the best all-around choice: It will smother weeds, convert insoluble phosphorus to a form that crops can absorb, and reach blossoming size in 30 days (when it is ready to incorporate into the soil). Even northern gardeners can get two crops in one season.

Other fast-growing grasses are annual ryegrass, barley, brome grass, millet, oats, Sudan grass or sorghum, wheat, and winter rye.

Canola, kale, and mustard, members of **the brassica family,** also make good green manure. These fast-growing, cool-season crops can be planted in spring or fall. Their massive root systems extend deep into the subsoil, and their decayed remains amend it. Incorporate them into the soil earlier in the season for nitrogen and later for organic matter.

Can't choose? Plant a legume and a grass together: Vetch and rye or peas and oats are common choices. Plus, a mix provides food and habitat, attracting a wide range of beneficial insects.

PLANTING AFTER COVER CROPS

The benefits of digging in green manure vary with a

crop's maturity.

A young crop decomposes quickly and releases minerals immediately yet provides little organic matter. Allow about 2 weeks before planting vegetables.

A midseason crop is harder to dig in, decomposes more slowly, and provides organic matter; however, its nutrients may be temporarily unavailable due to soil microbes that are digesting it. Once the microbes die, the nutrients become available to plantings that follow. Allow at least 4 weeks before planting vegetables.

A mature crop decomposes and releases nutrients slowly but provides the most organic matter. Allow 6 to 8 weeks before planting vegetables.

Cover crops that are allowed to go to seed will reseed themselves and become a nuisance. In the old days,

EASY GREEN EFFECTS

• Plant dwarf white clover or vetch between rows of anything to add nitrogen to the soil during the growing season.

• Underplant green manure grass around a main crop (e.g., seed buckwheat around established squash plants) to suppress weeds. Cut it in 4 to 6 weeks and use the clippings as mulch.

gardeners were encouraged to till and dig the soil (remember double digging?). The prevailing wisdom is to avoid disturbing soil layers.

Choose your method:

Mow or chop down cover crops or cut them with a string trimmer. Then, dig them into the topsoil.

Pull up cover crops by hand and use them as mulch. Kill tough plants (rye and vetch) by cutting them off at the crown. Then, lay them over the roots. Eventually, they will decompose, roots and all, and return their nutrients to the soil.

After being cut down, some cover crops (e.g., Sudan grass, winter barley, and winter rye) exude compounds that indiscriminately prevent seeds from germinating: They can affect vegetables (beets, carrots, chard, lettuce, radishes, spinach) as well as weeds. To avoid crop failure, use transplants with two to four leaves and follow green manure (e.g., winter rye) with late-season crops such as corn or squash, after the manure's growth-suppressing toxins have dissipated.

MY FERTILIZER RECORD

DATE	VEGETABLE	FERTILIZER	NOTES

MY FERTILIZER RECORD

DATE	VEGETABLE	FERTILIZER	NOTES

HOW TO SAVE SEEDS

A SEED KNOWS HOW TO WAIT . . . A SEED
IS ALIVE WHILE IT WAITS.
–Hope Jahren, scientist, author of Lab Girl *(b. 1969)*

Gardeners tend to be a thrifty lot, and saving seeds from one year to the next just makes sense. But there are three other good reasons to learn the techniques:

■ **Saving seeds ensures that you'll always have seeds of a favorite variety.** This is important; varieties are disappearing at an alarming rate. Just because you've been able to order a special seed variety from a commercial source in the past doesn't mean that it will always be available.

■ **Saving seeds is cost-effective.** Why spend money to buy seeds, or at least those of your favorite annual vegetables? (Biennials, such as cabbages, require space and time, so continue buying those.)

■ **Saving seeds opens you to the world of seed-trading.** Many of the vegetable varieties being grown today have no commercial sources.

If you'd like to try them, you have to trade seeds that you have for seeds that you want.

Here's how to gather and treat seeds from commonly grown vegetables.

SAVE SELECTIVELY

Save seeds only from open-pollinated or heirloom varieties, never from hybrids. An open-pollinated plant is one whose offspring replicate the parents. That is, its seeds will breed true to type. This is not so with modern hybrids, which are produced by crossing two or more inbred varieties to obtain specific characteristics. If you save seeds from a hybrid, the next generation will have unpredictable traits. You likely will not have the same variety that you originally planted.

For successful seed-saving, you must ensure seed purity. This means that plants that readily crossbreed among their own varieties (such as

cucumbers, peppers, melons, and squashes) need to be isolated from other varieties of that particular vegetable by distance, caging, bagging, or other means. If you're a beginner, just grow one variety of these at a time.

HOW TO KNOW WHEN A SEED IS RIPE

Ripeness is when the seeds are viable, which is not necessarily always when the plant is most edible. With the exception of tomatoes, pick your seed crops as late into the season as possible. Seeds attached to the parent fruit receive nourishment until harvest. Always harvest peas, beans, and lettuce seeds in dry weather. This speeds up the drying process and prevents mold.

Beans and peas are ready when the pods turn brown on the vine and shrink against the seeds. Pick the dry brown pods from the vines and remove the seeds; these will

require additional air-drying. One way is to put them into loosely woven baskets and stir them once a day. Typically, it takes about 6 weeks of air-drying for the seeds to be fully dry. If frost or other inclement weather threatens legumes that are ripe but not dry, pull up the vines by the roots and hang the plants upside down in a warm area, such as a basement, garage, outbuilding, or barn. The pods will draw energy from

the plants for another few days, which will increase the seed viability.

Other pod plants: **Radishes, lettuce,** and **Chinese greens** also produce seeds in pods after the plant has flowered. It is best to let the pods dry on the plant. However, these plants tend to dry from the bottom up, a few pods at a time. The dry ones are prone

to shattering and spreading their seeds all over the ground, so either bag the seed heads (put a paper bag tied at the base over the plants to capture the seeds; old nylons or row-cover materials let you see how the seeds are doing) or pick the dry pods daily.

Pepper seeds are ripe when peppers are at their full color (depending on variety, this could be red, orange, yellow, purple, or black) and start to shrivel. Cut peppers open to find the seeds in a mass on the central stem. Brush them off the stem onto a plate or screen and put them aside to dry.

Cucumber seeds are ripe when the cuke turns fully yellow, or overripe for eating. Harvest it and put it in a safe place for another 20 days. Cucumbers (and tomatoes) have seeds that are coated with a gel containing antigermination compounds.

Tomato seeds are ripe when tomatoes are firm but tender. If you press them, they have some give, unlike the hard feel that you get with green ones. Like peppers, they will also have reached their full color.

Just like cucumber seeds, tomato seeds are coated with a gel containing anti-germination compounds. The gel must be removed by fermentation to successfully save these seeds. In addition to removing the gel, fermentation kills many seedborne pathogens, ensuring disease-free seeds. The process smells bad, however, so don't do it in an enclosed room in the house.

Follow these steps for **tomatoes** and **cucumbers:** Squeeze or spoon the seed mass into a waterproof container (e.g., clear-plastic cup, jar, water glass, or deli

A SPEEDY WAY TO TOMATO SEEDS

Take seeds from your best open-pollinated specimens, smear the pulpy mix onto brown paper bags, and let the bags dry in the hot sun. When all of the moisture has evaporated, the seeds may be removed and stored in a cool, dry place for planting the following spring.

–Strawbery Banke, a living history museum in Portsmouth, New Hampshire

container). Add enough water to equal the volume of the seed mass and place the container in a warm spot out of direct sunlight. Stir the contents at least once a day. In a couple of days, the fermentation process will have started. Viable seeds will sink to the bottom, and bad seeds, debris from the seed mass, and a white mold will float on the surface. When all of the good seeds have dropped (which takes about 5 days), rinse away the gunk on top. Wash the seeds in several changes of water and lay them out in a single layer on a paper towel, glass or plastic plate, or screen. Put the seeds in a warm place until

they are fully dry; this can take several weeks.

Squash: **Winter squash** seeds are ripe when the skin turns hard. When squashes are ready, break them open and remove the seeds. Hold the seeds under running water, rubbing them between your fingers to remove any stringy material and membrane. Then lay them out on a plate or screen to dry. **Summer squash** seeds are ripe when the squash is past the edible point, with a hard rind. Then treat the same as winter squashes.

HOW TO KNOW WHEN A SEED IS DRY

To test if seeds are fully dried, squeeze one with pliers or hit it with a hammer. If it's dry, it will shatter. If it just crushes or feels soft or spongy, then your seeds still need more air-drying before being stored.

HOW TO STORE SEEDS

Once your seeds are completely dry, they can be stored in any suitable, airtight containers (e.g., pill bottles) and kept in a cool, dry, dark area.

Seeds will remain viable for up to 15 years, depending on type. You can extend their viability by freezing them, especially if you have a zero-degree freezer. Properly dried and frozen seeds will remain viable for at least 40 years.

MY SEED-SAVING RECORD

DATE	SOURCE/VARIETY	PLANTING NOTES

MY SEED-SAVING RECORD

DATE	SOURCE/VARIETY	PLANTING NOTES

MY SEED-SAVING RECORD

DATE	SOURCE/VARIETY	PLANTING NOTES

CROP ROTATION

ONE OF THE WORST MISTAKES THAT YOU CAN MAKE AS
A GARDENER IS TO THINK THAT YOU'RE IN CHARGE.
–Janet Gillespie, American garden writer (1913–2005)

Many beginning gardeners (and some long-timers) do not realize (or want to admit) that repeating a plot plan over consecutive years by growing annual vegetables in the same place results in plants that fail to thrive and a harvest that declines from one year to the next. Often, blame falls on bugs, diseases, bad weather, bad timing, bad soil, even bad karma.

While these factors may be at play, many times the culprit is bad habit: Failure to rotate crops. If this sounds like you, here's what to do.

Draw a plot plan of your most recent vegetable garden. Write in the types of vegetables that grew in each area.

This record is critical. Where you plant in one growing season dictates where you plant in the next. The core principle of crop rotation is planting annual vegetables based on their botanical family. Plants in the same family are genetically related and thus share similar characteristics (leaf appearance and/or tendrils for climbing, for example).

WHY ROTATE CROPS?
When performed properly, crop rotation brings many benefits . . .

■ **Fewer insect pests and** soilborne diseases: Plants with family ties are vulnerable to the same pests and diseases. When overwintering insects that live in the soil come looking for last year's host vegetables, they won't find any members of the plant family.

■ **Improved soil nutrition:** Some plants add nutrients to the soil, while others extract nutrients.

■ **Better soil structure:** Deep-rooted plants penetrate and break up the subsoil, allowing air and water in. They also draw up trace minerals and needed nutrients.

In the accompanying chart, you'll find annual vegetables and some herbs sorted by family name (both common and Latin).

ROTATION BASICS
The practice of crop rotation requires that vegetable crops in the same family not be planted in the same place/s (or same soil, if you're using pots) every year. The vegetable

TECHNOLOGY TO THE RESCUE
If you do not have a plot plan of your last garden, are beginning a garden from scratch, or find the plant families baffling, leave it to technology: *The Old Farmer's Almanac* Garden Planner, for desktop or laptop, will tell you what to plant where this year and every year; it saves the plot maps! Go to Almanac.com/gardenplanner for details.

family must rotate together. However, it is not necessary to grow every family or every plant in each family.

Rotation schedules vary in complexity. A few sources advise putting 2 years between same-site plantings; most recommend at least 3, ideally 4 (see box on page 194), or, depending on the size of your garden and desired harvest, even more years, adding cover crops (see pages 182–183) to the cycle.

Consider the size of your plot and the plants that you want. For a very small garden, try a 3-year plot, where you could grow legumes (pea family) in the first year, tomatoes and other nightshade plants in the next year, and gourds in the third year. The fourth year brings you back to legumes to repeat the cycle. Alternatively, these three families could also be planted in three separate plots in the first year and rotated in this order in ensuing years.

PLAN YOUR NEXT GARDEN
Make a list of the vegetables that you want to grow, keeping the family members together based on the chart.

Develop a garden plan based on the family groups and the multiyear rotation examples above.

If this is a new garden, designate an area for each

SELECTED VEGETABLES AND HERBS

FAMILY	MEMBERS
Carrot, aka Parsley (Apiaceae, aka Umbelliferae)	caraway, carrot*, celeriac, celery, chervil, cilantro, dill, fennel, lovage, parsley, parsnip
Goosefoot, aka Chard (Chenopodiaceae)	beet*, orache, quinoa, spinach, Swiss chard
Gourd, aka Squash (Cucurbitaceae)	cucumber, gourd, melon, pumpkin, squash (summer and winter), watermelon
Grass (Poaceae, aka Gramineae)	sweet corn
Mallow (Malvaceae)	okra
Mint (Lamiaceae, aka Labiatae)	anise hyssop, basil, Chinese artichoke, lavender, mint, oregano, rosemary, sage, summer savory, sweet marjoram, thyme
Morning Glory (Convolvulaceae)	sweet potato
Mustard, aka Cabbage (Brassicaceae, aka Cruciferae)	arugula, bok choy, broccoli, brussels sprouts, cabbage, cauliflower, collard, kale, kohlrabi, komatsuna, mizuna, mustard greens, radish*, rutabaga, turnip, watercress
Nightshade (Solanaceae)	eggplant, pepper, potato, tomatillo, tomato
Onion (Amaryllidaceae*)	chives, garlic, leek, onion, shallot
Pea, aka Legume (Fabaceae, aka Leguminosae)	bush, kidney, lima, pole, and soy beans; lentil; pea; peanut
Sunflower, aka Aster (Asteraceae, aka Compositae)	artichoke (globe and Jerusalem), calendula, chamomile, dandelion, endive, escarole, lettuce, radicchio, salsify, sunflower, tarragon

These can be planted among any family.

plant family. Keep the design simple.

If you are introducing crop rotation into an existing garden, identify the plant families in your garden. With luck, some family members will be clustered.

However, if your last garden was a riotous arrangement of scattered plants, you have a few options: You could begin a new garden; amend the soil of the existing plot with a cover crop and grow vegetables next season; or choose a limited number of plant families that you want to grow again, note where they grew last year, and plan to grow and rotate families more or less within those spaces.

Crop rotation may sound like it's complicated and quite a bit of work (remember, there's always our Garden Planner app to do it for you!). But if you spend a little time considering past and future plot plans now, things will begin to make sense and save you a lot of time and cents later.

> **GET INSPIRED BY GARDENS! FOLLOW US ON**
> 📷 **@THEOLDFARMERSALMANAC**

FOUR X FOUR: 4 PLOTS, 4 YEARS

A 4-year rotation could be four plots, rows, or quarters of a circle, with a different plant family in each one. For example, in plot or row one, the mustard family; in the next plot or row, the nightshade or gourd family; in the third, the carrot or onion family; and in the fourth, the pea family. Every year, the plant families would move to the next plot, always in that order.

MY ROTATION RECORD

DATE	VARIETY	LOCATION

MY ROTATION RECORD

DATE	VARIETY	LOCATION

MY ROTATION RECORD

DATE	VARIETY	LOCATION

INDOOR GARDENING

ONE OF THE MOST DELIGHTFUL THINGS ABOUT
A GARDEN IS THE ANTICIPATION THAT IT PROVIDES.
—*W. E. Johns, English writer (1893–1968)*

Indoor gardening enables you to have fresh edibles throughout the dormant days of winter until it's time to grow outdoors or even year-round, especially if outdoor gardening is not an option. Indoor techniques and technology abound. Elaborate hydroponic systems, expensive mini-greenhouses, and other pieces of equipment and technology are available for those who want to garden indoors on a large scale; we favor simple (although not necessarily small) methods for growing microgreens and herbs.

THE WINDOW GARDEN
Whether you live in a Chicago high-rise or Montana log cabin, as long as you have a south-facing window and time, you can garden indoors all year long with minimal investment in equipment and maximum benefit to your culinary efforts.

You will need:
- **Bright light.** A south-facing window with 6+ hours of direct winter sun works best. Supplement, if needed, with a strip of grow lights (see next page).
- **Water.** If your tap water is heavily chlorinated, you might want to buy springwater for your plants. To avoid overwatering, set pots and trays on pebble-filled pans so that water can drain off.
- **Containers.** To grow microgreens indoors, use shallow trays or pans with drainage holes. You need only 1 to 2 inches of soil because the plants will not be growing to full size. For herbs, choose a pot that's a minimum of 8 inches deep, with a drainage hole in the bottom.
- **Soil.** Use a fertile, light-texture, potting mix or seed-starting medium. Do not use garden soil. If your potting soil seems clumpy, mix in some vermiculite to lighten it.

- **Spray bottle** to moisten soil; this works better than a watering can.
- **Plastic wrap** to cover seed-starting containers.

Sow the seeds (read the seed packet for depth and coverage).

Spray to moisten the soil now and as needed; keep the soil merely damp, not soggy, to avoid damping-off disease (see page 47).

Cover the pot or tray with a loose layer of plastic wrap to conserve humidity. Check it at least once a day, and remove the plastic as soon as the seeds begin to sprout.

Use a well-diluted liquid fertilizer every 2 to 3 weeks for microgreens and annual herbs. Use it on perennial herbs in the spring to encourage them.

Rotate trays and pots of seedlings each day for upright growth.

Harvest microgreens when they are about 2 inches high,

using scissors to cut a few stems near the soil line. Do not uproot the whole plant. Greens will regrow.

Start new trays of microgreens at 2- to 3-week intervals for a steady supply.

A MICRO MENU

Microgreens vary widely in flavors, colors, and textures, from smooth green and red lettuces to beets, kale, spinach, Swiss chard, spicy mustard greens, and peppery arugula. Consider seed packs of mixed microgreens (often labeled "mesclun"); these different greens can be harvested at the same time.

Green onions have shallow-growing root systems and don't require much space (a 4- to 5-inch-deep container). Water regularly, whenever the top of the soil feels dry. Harvest the tops by cutting 1 to 2 inches above the soil, so that the little roots will grow another head of greens.

Herbs basil and cilantro sprout in as few as 5 days and can be reseeded for succession plantings in any season.

Parsley, dill, and marjoram take more than 3 weeks to sprout; consider purchasing seedlings, if time is a concern.

Perennial herbs such as chives, mint, rosemary, and sage can last indoors for several years if they are kept trimmed. Although they may lose vigor in winter air and light, they can usually be coaxed through the season, or you can take cuttings and start fresh in spring.

SOME ENLIGHTENMENT ABOUT GROW LIGHTS

The grow-light options are wide-ranging, from fluorescent to HID (high-intensity discharge) to LED (light-emitting diode). Each type has an array of power requirements, brightness levels, and color temperatures.

Compact Fluorescent Lamp (CFL) Lights, aka common household fluorescents, are an effective supplement to natural (window) light. When starting seeds, use a "full-spectrum" fluorescent bulb made specifically for fruiting or flowering plants. For best results, place the bulb in a directional lamp 3 to 6 inches above the plant(s).

High-Intensity Discharge (HID) Lights are ideal for growing maturing edible plants. However, HIDs are expensive, use electricity inefficiently, and give off heat. Despite this, they are widely used in plant nurseries and large-scale grow houses because of their raw power.

Light-Emitting Diode (LED) Lights: For efficiently growing large numbers of plants, full-spectrum LEDs provide the best results. They use significantly less power to produce more light than traditional CFLs, and they produce very little heat. Although LEDs are more expensive than fluorescent bulbs, the LED lifetime is far longer.

Before you purchase grow lights, decide how many plants you want to illuminate and how much area they will occupy under the light(s). This will enable you to calculate how many bulbs you'll need.

Think about how to position the light(s) over the plants so that you can easily alter the distance between the lights and the plants as they grow. Common options include suspending the lights from chains above your plants (e.g., on the ceiling or a sawhorse) and adjusting the chains as the plants grow. Or, stabilizing the light(s) and setting the planters on a stack of books, removing volumes as needed to lower the maturing plants.

Remember, too, that each type of grow light provides a different amount of light. To be most effective, each light should be a specific distance from the plants: Fluorescent lights should be 3 to 12 inches above the tops of the plants; HIDs, 24 to 60 inches; and LEDs, 12 to 24 inches.

Plants grown under lights indoors need more hours of light than the same plants do outdoors. Grow lights should be on for at least 14 but no more than 18 hours per day; even indoor plants need a minimum of 6 hours of darkness each day.

MY CONTAINER-GARDEN RECORD

DATE	VARIETY	NOTES

OBSERVATIONS AND REMINDERS

ABOUT MY GARDEN

OBSERVATIONS AND REMINDERS

CHANGES TO MAKE NEXT YEAR

_____

_____

_____

_____

_____

_____

_____

_____

_____

_____

_____

_____

_____

_____

_____

OBSERVATIONS AND REMINDERS

ABOUT MY GARDEN

OBSERVATIONS AND REMINDERS

CHANGES TO MAKE NEXT YEAR

INDEX

Note: **Boldface** references
indicate tables.

A
Alfalfa meal, 178
Animal pest control, 168–169
Anise, 58
Anthracnose, 158
Aphids, 54, 59, 60, 61, 85, 111,
162
Aragonite, 28
Asparagus, **34,** 68–70, **181**
beetles, 162
rust, 161
Azomite, 29

B
Basil, 58–59
Bean(s), **34,** 56, 71–73, **174,
181**
common mosaic virus, 160
seed-saving, 186–187
Beetles
asparagus, 162
Colorado potato, 163
cucumber, 163
flea, 164
Japanese, 164
Mexican bean, 164
Beets, **34,** 74–75, **174, 181**
Bell peppers, **34,** 123–124,
175, 181
seed-saving, 187–188
Black canker, 158
Black rot, 158
Blight, early, 159
Blight, late, 159
Blood meal, 178
Blossom-end rot, 159
Bone char, 29
Borage, 59
Borers, squash vine, 165
Broccoli, **34,** 76–77, **174, 181**
Brussels sprouts, **34,** 78–79,
174, 181

C
Cabbage, **34,** 80–82, **174, 181**
loopers, 162
moths, 163
root maggots, 163
whites, 163

-worms, imported, 163
Calcium, 28, 29, 178
Calphos colloidal phosphate,
29
Carrot(s), **34,** 83–84, **174, 181**
rust flies, 163
Cauliflower, **34,** 85–86, **174,
181**
Celery, **34,** 87–89, **174, 181**
Cercospora leaf spot, 160
Chard, Swiss, 34, 145–146
Chives, 59–60
Cilantro, 60
Clubroot, 159
Collards, pH for, **34**
Colorado potato beetles, 163
Comfrey, 179
Companion plants, 54–56, **55**
three sisters, 56
Compost, 20, 36–37
hot, how to make, 36–37
tea, how to make, 180–181
Container(s)
diseases, soilborne, 22
*See also individual diseases
and 158–162*
for seed-starting, 45
grow bag, 25
indoor, 198
pests, and, 22
*See also individual pests
and 162–166*
plants for, 24, 25
potting mix recipe, 25
self-watering, 24
size(s), **24, 25**
soil, 24, **25**
types of, 22–23, 25
wood for, 22
Container gardening, 22–25,
198–200
Coriander, 60
Corn, **34,** 56, 90–92, **174, 181**
earworms, 163
rootworms, southern, 163
Cover crops, 182–183
Cracking, 159
Critter-proofing, 168–169
Crop rotation, 192–194

vegetable and herb families,
193
Cucumber(s), **34,** 93–95, **174,
181**
beetles, 163
mosaic virus, 160
seed-saving, 188
Cultivating crops, 170–171
Cutworms, 163

D
Damping off, 47
Dill, 60–61
Diseases, 158–162
See also individual diseases
Downy mildew, 160
Drip lines, 173

E
Earthworm soil test, 27
Earwigs, European, 164
Edamame, **34,** 96–97
Eggplant, **34,** 98–100, **181**
Equipment and tools, 10,
14–15, 173

F
Fertilize, when to, **181**
Fertilizer(s), 17–19, 176–183
brassica family, 182
comfrey, 179
compost tea, 180–181
cover crops, 182–183
grains, 182
granular, 177
grasses, 182
legumes, 182
organic, 176
seaweed, 176
soluble, 177–178
stinging nettle, 179
synthetic, 176–177
tea, 179–180
Fish meal, 178
Flea beetles, 164
Footprint test, 52
French tarragon, 64
Frost dates, 11, **12, 13**
Fruitworms, tomato, 163
Fusarium crown rot, 159
Fusarium wilt, 160, 161

INDEX

PHOTO CREDITS